ACROSS THE WAVES

First published in 2002 by Mercier Press
Douglas Village Cork
Tel: (021) 489 9858; Fax: (021) 489 9887
Email: books@mercierpress.ie
16 Hume Street Dublin 2
Tel: (01) 661 5299; Fax: (01) 661 8583
E.mail: books@marino.ie
Web: www.mercier.ie

Trade enquiries to CMD Distribution
55A Spruce Avenue
Stillorgan Industrial Park
Blackrock County Dublin
Tel: (01) 294 2560; Fax: (01) 294 2565
E.mail: cmd@columba.ie

© T. Ryle Dwyer 2002

ISBN 1 85635 347 8
10 9 8 7 6 5 4 3 2 1

A CIP record for this title is available
from the British Library.

Cover design by Mercier Press
Set in Goudy
Printed in Ireland by ColourBooks
Baldoyle Industrial Estate Dublin 13

to Malcolm and Kristin

ACROSS THE WAVES

T. RYLE DWYER

MERCIER PRESS

Contents

Author's Introduction

One of my mother's earliest memories was of her American father warning her Irish-born mother that they would probably be jailed because she had helped illegal immigrants from her home town of Tralee. He had just learned that one of those young men was a fugitive, recently escaped from Owego State Penitentiary, where he had been serving time for illegal immigration. My grandmother was a warm-hearted woman who spoke her mind. When I mentioned to my Great-aunt Gerty that my grandmother believed that their father was an alcoholic, she reacted with horror. I doubt that she would have been more shocked if I had shot her. She took a deep breath and sat bolt upright. 'Well, she told you much too much for you own good!' Gerty exclaimed. If she were alive to read this book, my great-aunt would probably hold that opinion more firmly than ever. Although my grandmother believed that her father, Thomas Ryle – after whom I was named – was an alcoholic, this did not mean she loved or admired him any the less. In fact, she blamed her mother's parents for interfering. That was probably far too simplistic a view, but it was what she thought, and she believed in saying what she thought. For six years, I had dinner at my grandmother's home every school day, as she lived within a stone's throw of the school. She had spent over fifty years in the United States and frequently lamented the fact that she had returned home. My mother recalled, however, that her mother, while she was living in the United States, had also constantly bemoaned the fact that she was missing life in Ireland.

Growing up in the south-west of Ireland in the 1950s, there was no television, so films were a popular form of entertainment. There was no shortage of movies about the Second World War, in which my father had been killed in action. Those films usually ended with the boys coming home, and my brother Seán and I became acutely aware that my mother would usually be crying at that point. Although nobody ever told us that we should not mention the war, in our own ways we learned not to do so.

My father's wartime letters were in the attic for over forty years until I retrieved them a few years ago and read through them in order for the first time. There was a problem in following his story once he went overseas, because all his letters from the front were marked as having come simply from 'Somewhere in France', 'Germany', 'Belgium' or 'Luxembourg'. Nonetheless, I was able to piece together that part of the story by tracing the progress of his regiment, with the aid of some books on the Second World War, especially John Colby's *War from the Ground Up: The 90th Division in WWII* (1991), which traced the movements of the division's four regiments.

My mother had some particularly interesting experience working as a radio-telephone operator, though she never mentioned her work in her letters, because it was highly confidential. This work included listening in to the early wartime conversations of Franklin Roosevelt and Winston Churchill, hearing the frantic calls of American soldiers telephoning from the Philippines as they were about to surrender to Japanese forces, and listening to the horrific reports of the Allied disaster at Dieppe. There were also the salacious titbits of information that telephone operators often picked up in the course of their work.

In one of my father's last letters, written just over a month before he was killed in Germany, he expressed the hope that the family might move to Ireland for a time after the war. My mother decided on such visit in 1948, and Tralee has been her home ever since. In that time, I have never heard her – unlike my grandmother – express any regret about the move. My mother's mother and paternal grandparents were among the hundreds of thousands of Irish people who emigrated to the United States in the century following the Great Famine, but my mother was one of the few Americans who brought her family in the other direction. This book is really the story of her life on both sides of the Atlantic.

TRD, Tralee

1

A TRALEE BACKGROUND

Mary Josephine Ryle, who was born in Tralee on 28 May 1888, was the first child of Thomas and Hanora Ryle. They had married the previous year. Thomas's parents had died young, leaving him their pub in Bridge Street, Tralee. His mother, Mary Lawlor, had emigrated to the United States, where she married a man named O'Donoghue. They had a child, but O'Donoghue died and Mary decided to return to Ireland, leaving the child with the O'Donoghue family in Boston. She then married a Tom Ryle and they had four sons. The youngest of these, Paddy, went out to join his half-brother in Boston, and lost touch with his family in Ireland. One of his daughters, Sister Reginald Ryle, a Dominican nun, re-established contact with the Irish side of the family in the 1950s.

Maurice Ryle, a brother of Thomas Ryle, became a journalist and established his own local newspaper, the *Kerry Sentinel*, before going on to take up a reporting position in the House of Commons in London. He later returned to Ireland and became editor of the *Evening Herald* and subsequently joint editor of the *Irish In-*

dependent. One of his granddaughters became famous as the singer Dusty Springfield, and another granddaughter, Barbara Nugent, became publisher of the *Sunday Tribune* and later the *Sunday Business Post*. Maurice's brothers Tom and Willy remained in Tralee. As the eldest son, Tom inherited the family pub. While still only twenty, he married Hanora McQuinn, the teenage daughter of a local well-to-do butcher. The McQuinns owned two butcher shops in Tralee, one in Upper Castle Street, across from St John's Parish Church, and the other in Bridge Street, near the densely populated Abbey area.

Tom Ryle was an active sportsman, playing both rugby and Gaelic football, and he was also a proficient handball player. As a young man with his own pub, he tended to be a rather free spirit – much to the disapproval of his wife's family. They compelled him to emigrate to the United States, to work there for a while, in order 'to get some sense'. It was a measure of how much influence the McQuinns had on the family that he went to the United States, leaving his young wife and daughter behind. He did not stay in America for very long, however, quietly returning to Ireland as quickly as he could. He stayed with relatives of his late mother between Farranfore and Killarney. At various times, he would sneak into town to be with his wife. When she learned that she was pregnant again, her parents willingly accepted Tom's return. Rightly or wrongly, Mary always believed that the interference of her mother's family had put her father under undue pressure, which was compounded by a growing family. In all, Tom and Hanora had seven daughters and one son. One of the daughters died in infancy, putting further strain on the family.

As they lived over their own pub, there was never a shortage of drink. One of Mary's earliest memories was, as a six-year-old, giving alcohol to her young sister Hannah, whom the family called Nance. Suddenly her mother realised that three-year-old Nance was drunk, and Mary fled to the home of her uncle Maurice Ryle for the day. He eventually brought her home and protected her by putting the blame squarely on Mary's parents for not watching her. She was too young to know the real implications of drink, he said. Amid the pressures of his life, Tom became one of his own best customers and, in the process, undermined his business. Mary blamed the interference of her mother's family for many of her father's problems. Her grandparents were tough people. In later life she would recall talking with them. They had lived through the Great Famine, but they never mentioned it. Mary therefore concluded that there was probably so much fish available in Tralee Bay and off the coast that the famine had not actually affected the town.

Lord John Russell, the British prime minister, acted as though the great mass of the Irish people could eat grass after the potato crop failed in the mid-1840s. Ignoring impassioned pleas from Irish civil servants in 1846, he issued instructions that the state should not purchase food from the United States, nor interfere with the export of foodstuffs from Ireland. The government also ordered that no new relief work should be started and, where such work was already in progress, the workers should be paid significantly less than those in regular employment. In addition, relief committees were told to sell food only 'at such a price as would cover all expenses for cost and carriage.' The failure of the potato crop in 1846 was almost total, and that winter turned out to be the coldest in living memory. That people remained quiet and orderly was 'a miracle', according to the *Kerry Examiner* on 20 October 1846. 'There is a wonderfully striking likeness between the social condition of this country at the present moment and that of France before the revolution,' the paper reported.

There were many acts of genuine charity, but the press recorded very little other than monetary contributions to relief committees. On 12 November 1846, some two months before the introduction of the Soup Kitchens Bill, relief committees in Tralee and Killarney set up 'soup shops' that sold soup at a penny a quart for the benefit of the starving. People who donated money were allowed to purchase tickets for distribution at half price. The *Kerry Evening Post* complained that this was financially imprudent, because some people might buy more tickets than the value of their contributions, and this would mean that the extra tickets would end up costing the committee money. Robert Hickson, a Tralee merchant, offered to sell a cargo of American wheat to the local relief committee, but he insisted on being paid more than the going rate. The committee therefore bought the wheat in Cork instead. A Tralee girl asked for help at the home of a gentleman, who checked out her tale of woe by going to her home, where he found the unshrouded corpse of a child on the table, where it had been for five days, because the family did not have the price of a coffin. The distressed mother was pressing another child, almost dead from the cold, to her bosom, to try to warm its body.

Twenty-one people died in the Tralee workhouse during the second week of December 1846; this exceeded the number of deaths in any two months since the workhouse was opened. Two weeks later, the death rate rose to twenty-nine. In January 1847, the Reverend Matthew T. Moriarty of Ventry witnessed the conditions in Skibbereen, County Cork, which is usually depicted as the place hardest hit by the famine, but he contended that conditions around Dingle were even worse. 'I have no hesitation in asserting that the parish of Ventry is worse off than Skibbereen, or any other part of Ireland,' he wrote.

'A poor woman and her three children left Dingle for Tralee to seek relief in the workhouse when every other source had failed. Faintness from want of food overcame the wretched creature and she had to lie down,' the *Kerry Evening Post* reported on 19 December 1846. In a short time, a passer-by found this hapless group, 'the mother dead and the children, whom she must have starved herself to feed, crying over the remains of their parent.' By March, an average of forty people were dying each week in the Tralee workhouse, which housed 1,300 people, even though it had been built to hold 800. 'Our streets are thronged with beggars, pale emaciated creatures hardly able to drag their limbs after them,' the *Kerry Evening Post* reported. 'The great mass of destitution that meets one at every corner is not of the Tralee poor, but of strangers recently driven here by destitution, which is further increased by the numbers who come to the workhouse for relief, and are refused admittance from the overcrowded state of the house.'

'I saw five children lying on the flags, and a more emaciated and famine-stricken group could not be conceived,' one reporter observed in Denny Street, Tralee. Three of the children leaned against a wall, as they could not stand or move without assistance. They showed little sign of life except for an occasional listless movement of the eyes. The other two could walk, but they were not much better. One child's hand had been so badly burned that a doctor who saw the wound said, 'It was useless to torture the wretched object with any attempt at cure, which would only inflict more pain on the poor sufferer.' In the doctor's opinion, the child would be better off dead. The five children were orphans from Dingle. They had struggled to get to the workhouse in Tralee, only to be refused admission because it was already overcrowded. 'A more fitting case for workhouse relief could not offer itself than that of those poor orphans,' the *Kerry Evening Post* lamented. 'Should not the guardians there have the power to make an exception in such an extreme case?'

The price of meat remained constant throughout the famine, which indicated that there was no shortage of meat for those who had the money to buy it. With two butcher shops, the McQuinns would have been particularly well off in that regard, but their later silence about the famine conditions may well have reflected the sense of guilt which is common among survivors of such tragedies.

As hardened individuals who had come through so much, the McQuinns probably had little understanding of the difficulties of their son-in-law, who was failing to make a go of the business that he had inherited. He lost the pub and had the indignity of being evicted with his wife and children, because he was unable to pay his debts. In the midst of such domestic unrest, Mary was not a particularly good student, while her sister Nora, who was a little over a year younger than her, was a model child. She was a brilliant student who won scholarships. She entered the convent and became a nun, spending much of her life in Australia.

In all, Mary had six sisters and one brother, Tommy. The youngest girl, Josephine, died as a three-year-old. Religion obviously played a major role in the family, as their mother followed a rather militant form of Catholicism that was tainted with a strong Jansenistic streak. The family used to say the Rosary together, and each night the mother called on them to pray that 'God would take Tommy to Himself before he takes to drink.' This, of course, amounted to calling on all the children to pray that God would strike young Tommy dead if he ever tried to drink alcohol. Not surprisingly, he never did drink! But of course, his father drank enough for the whole family – or at least that was how his oldest daughter remembered it. He obviously did not share his wife's narrow Catholic views. He had been a fervent admirer of the Protestant leader of the Irish Parliamentary Party, Charles Stewart Parnell, who was undermined in the early 1890s when the news broke that he was having an affair with Kitty O'Shea, the wife of one of his colleagues. O'Shea had used the affair to secure political advancement for himself.

Even though Tom Ryle had a keen interest in politics, his daughter Mary grew up in a period in which politics was in the doldrums in Ireland. After finishing school, she got a job in Revington's drapery, where she trained as a dressmaker and ultimately as a coatmaker, which she always maintained required much more skill. She wanted to become a nurse, but her mother would not hear of her going to England, and they could not afford the fees for her to do nursing in Ireland. She therefore decided to go to the United States. Mary's paternal great-uncle Father Tom Lawlor, the parish priest of Killorglin, offered to provide the money for her passage to America, but he insisted that she had to have her mother's approval. Initially her mother would not hear of her emigrating, until Mary threatened to marry Georgie Johnson, a local Protestant. The fact that Georgie knew nothing of this was only incidental. He had never shown any interest in Mary, but the idea that she might marry a Protestant was too much for her mother. Mary therefore got her mother's blessing on her emigrating to avoid the scandal of a mixed marriage.

Mary emigrated to the United States in 1911 with her friend Anna Sheehan. By a quirk of fate, Georgie Johnson left Tralee the same day; Mary's mother fainted when she heard this. For days afterwards she felt ill at the thought that Mary had eloped with Georgie. When Mary's younger sister, Nance, wanted to go to England to do nursing during the First World War, her mother approved, only to have some of her worst fears realised. Nance married Leslie Frazer, a South African of Scottish extraction. He had three strikes against him as far as Nance's mother was concerned: he was not only a Protestant but also a soldier and, worse, fighting for the British. From what he had heard of his mother-in-law, he assumed he would not be welcome in Tralee, when he and Nance visited Ireland after the war. He stayed in Dublin, flatly refusing to go to Tralee unless Nance's mother invited him, but she refused. Her view was that he could come and he would not be made to feel unwelcome, but she was not going to invite him. Nance then made her home in South Africa.

Before emigrating, Mary Ryle was informally engaged to Dan O'Sullivan of Tralee. He was supposed to follow her out to the United States, where they would get married. Mary initially stayed with his sister, Nelly Lynch, in New York. Mary was so homesick at the time that she advised Dan to stay in Ireland, as she planned to return home as soon as possible. She obtained a job as a domestic servant at the home of a doctor. She was great with the doctor's children and was brilliant when it came to making or mending the family's clothes. As a result, the doctor took an interest in her development and arranged for her to enrol at the training school for nurses at Manhattan State Hospital, where she qualified as a State Registered Nurse in October 1914. One of the men she dated in those years was Steve Early, who later became a close aide to President Franklin D. Roosevelt.

While working as a nurse, Mary met Cornelius Joseph Harrigan, a first-generation Irish-American. Both of his parents were from Cork city. His father actually met Helen O'Sullivan on the boat going to the United States. She was a teenage girl emigrating with her whole family at the time. Shortly afterwards they got married in New York City, where he ran a livery stable, but he was killed when kicked in the head by a horse shortly before the birth of his fourth son, Connie, on 2 August 1894. Helen was left to raise the four boys – John, Joe, Mike and Connie – on her own. Their surname, Harrigan, possibly a corruption of Horgan, was a very uncommon name. It was popularised in 1907 by George M. Cohan with the song 'Harrigan'; this song later became a hit for Bing Crosby, whose mother's family name was also Harrigan, from Cork.

In fact, Connie gained a measure of success as a musical composer by having some sheet music published. He was working at the same hospital as Mary. For some reason he had obtained the job under his second name, Joseph, which was the name by which Mary got to know him. As a result, she always called him 'Joe', even though he was 'Connie' to his family. It seemed that 'Joseph' was a particularly popular name in the Harrigan household. In addition to the second son, Joe, each of the boys was given Joseph as his second name. Connie and Mary, whose second name was actually Josephine, got married on 2 September 1917. She was more than six years older than him, but she learned this only as they were signing the marriage register. She later stated that she would never have married him if she had known of the age gap between them. She was obviously afraid that people would accuse her of 'cradle-snatching'.

In addition to working at the hospital where he met Mary, Connie Harrigan worked for a bus company and later on the railway. He got jobs for a number of friends and acquaintances, including his best friend Charlie Klenke, whose Irish wife, Noni, was from Glin, County Limerick. They both tried to join the American army during the First World War, but Connie was rejected on health grounds. Klenke served with the American Expeditionary Force in Europe. Afterwards he served as a driver for the future president Herbert Hoover as the politician traveled around Belgium organising famine relief in 1919.

By this time, Mary and Connie had started a family. In all, they had four children, the first of whom, Margaret, was born on 6 October 1918. At the time, they were living next to the Church of St Jean Baptiste on Lexington Avenue and Seventy-sixth Street in New York City. This was the start of the Prohibition era, during which the sale and possession of alcohol was outlawed in the United States. Margaret later learned that a couple of enterprising youngsters regularly used her to transport liquor, unknown to herself or her parents, who would have been horrified if they had known at the time what was happening. Believing that her father was an alcoholic, Mary had a kind of aversion to the demon drink. Almost a quarter of a century later, during the Second World War, Margaret met a soldier in California who told an amazing story after learning that the two of them had had lived in the same apartment house on Lexington Avenue. Mike Hession recalled that 'a Mrs Harrigan' used to allow him and a friend to wheel the baby in a pram. This was shortly after the introduction of Prohibition. They would collect some bottles of booze from a supplier, hide them under the baby's blankets and deliver them in the neighbourhood without arousing any suspicion. Mary remembered young Hession and his friend McGucken asking to wheel the baby but had had no idea of what they were doing on the side.

A couple of years later, the Harrigans had a second daughter, Loretta, and the family moved to Seventy-fourth Street, where they lived in a large apartment house. Margaret's early memories of that building were of living across the way from the Hanley family. Frances and Kathleen were some years older than her but they sometimes took her downtown, where their father was head waiter in the Commodore Hotel. The children would be taken into the dining room by the staff and given ice cream, which was a real treat on the hot summer days.

Mary was aware of the developments in Ireland during the Black-and-Tan period (1920–21), but she had no understanding of the subsequent Civil War. Like most people in Tralee, her family sympathised with the republicans. Some of them fled to the United States and called on her for help. When Austin Stack visited New York in early 1922, collecting money for the newly formed Cumann na Poblachta ('Republican Association'), Mary served on a fund-raising committee for him. It was ironic, because she had known Stack in Tralee and had never liked him. She was friendly with a couple of his sisters but always considered him a bully. When Stack was looking for help in the United States, however, she was glad to assist, because he was a Tralee man. That was enough for Mary Harrigan; politics really had nothing to do with it. During the Civil War of 1922–23, her first cousin, Michael Ryle, was killed near Ballyseedy. Mary put up a number of republicans who fled to America during the short conflict and its aftermath. Those included Tommy Vale, John Carmody and Tim Fitzgerald, all from Tralee. Connie Harrigan got them jobs on the railway.

One night in the summer of 1924, Vale and Fitzgerald brought back another Tralee man, Pat 'Belty' Williams of Ashe Street. He had an amazing tale to tell. He had left Ireland in June, with the aim of going to Canada so that he could slip across the border into the United States on foot. It was not that difficult for Irish people to emigrate to the United States at the time, but they had to have somebody to sponsor them in America. Williams did not have a sponsor, but his brother Joe in Newfoundland had sent him the fare for the trip. On the train to Cobh, Belty teamed up with a republican from Clare who was planning to go to the United States by the same route. They sailed to Quebec and then travelled by train to a small town on the Canadian side of the border. They headed south on foot with just a compass. They walked until dawn, stopping only to eat a few sandwiches that they had brought with them. They then made their way to Chazy, New York, from where they tried to take a train to New York City, but two suspicious state troopers arrested them at the train station.

Williams admitted that they had entered the United States illegally. He gave a false name, William Wilson. The pair were taken to Albany, where they were sentenced to three months in the federal penitentiary in Owego, New York. On completion of their sentences, they were to be deported back to Ireland. Williams was determined to stay in America. He therefore set about escaping, with a young Jewish man from Liverpool who was in the same predicament. 'We noticed that the prison governor and his family took off for the country every Saturday,' Williams explained. 'We cultivated the friendliness of a trustee – a trusted prisoner near the end of his sentence. He was an Irish-American who did a lot of chores in the governor's house, which was adjacent to the jail. It was really part of the prison. An iron gate into the governor's garden was always locked, as the governor's house opened onto the street. As the house was likely to be empty for around six hours on Saturday, the escape was planned for then.'

With the help of others, a diversionary fight was organised in the prison yard. Williams and his Jewish friend had bribed the trustee to unlock the back gate to the governor's home for them. 'The whole thing turned out to be so simple,' Williams explained. 'When the "shindig" started, the attention of the guards was naturally diverted and we slipped through the unlocked gate and closed it behind us. We then walked through the garden and into the cellar of the governor's house, then up the cellar stairs. We opened the front door and walked casually into the quiet street. With our hearts thumping, we walked through the small town to find the railroad tracks.' Unlike Ireland, where there were many houses by the tracks, nobody lived beside the tracks in the countryside in upstate New York. The two men travelled for hours without having to stay clear of people. They took cover only when a train approached. After five hours they reached a small town, where they hitched a lift on a milk truck to Binghamton, about sixty miles from Owego. There they boarded the Montreal–New York train in the early hours of the next morning.

After arriving at Grand Central Station in New York City, they spent a couple of nights sleeping rough in Central Park. Williams telegraphed his brother in Newfoundland for money, which allowed the two of them to get a place to stay. He knew that his friend Tommy Vale was somewhere in New York City. He bought an Irish-American newspaper to get in touch with some Irish people and learned that there was a Kerry dance at a hall on Fifty-ninth Street and Eighth Avenue the following Saturday night. 'I found the dance hall and was hardly inside when I saw, dancing around, Tim Fitzgerald from Tralee,' Williams recalled years later. 'I wasted no time in literally separating him from his dance partner. There was a great look of astonishment on his face. Where did I come from? How did I get to New York, etc, etc?' Tommy Vale and John Carmody joined them later. They left the dance and adjourned to a restaurant, where they could talk more easily. Williams told them about his escape from Owego. They suggested that he should come back and stay with them for the weekend.

Margaret was not yet six years old at the time but she remembered these young Irishmen staying with them for short periods, especially Williams. He had a cloth cap, which he put on her backwards, and everybody remarked that she looked like the child film star Jackie Coogan. Her most abiding memory of Belty's stay, however, was her father's horror at the realisation that they were harbouring an escaped fugitive. 'May, we are going to end up in a penitentiary, and who is going to take the children?' Margaret heard her father say to her mother. Margaret did not know what a penitentiary was, but it certainly sounded scary, especially if she was going to be left alone. She never forgot the incident.

At the time, tuberculosis was a killer disease that people sought to hide. People were so afraid of it that they acted as if it was the same thing as terminal syphilis. Connie's eldest brother, John, a postal worker, had died of TB on 9 February 1922. It was thought that he brought it into the home, and his brother Joe and their mother also succumbed. In the circumstances, it was probably understandable that, after Connie was diagnosed with TB, his brother Mike was afraid to visit him. As a result, contact with the only surviving member of the family was lost.

In later life, when Bing Crosby expressed an interest in tracing his Harrigan relations, Mary would get many calls from the media about a possible family connection. For instance, when she retired back home to Ireland in the 1950s, she was the only Harrigan in the telephone directory for the whole country. Every time Crosby came to Ireland, reporters would call her, but she really knew very little about her late husband's family and apparently could not have cared less after the way his only surviving brother had refused to visit him as he was dying. It must have been a particularly trying time for Mary Harrigan. A third child, Mary, was born in September 1923 but she had serious birth defects and never really had a chance. She died before her first birthday, but then Loretta became seriously ill and Margaret was sent away to Nanuet, New York, to a boarding school, which she hated. While she was away, Loretta died of TB peritonitis. In 1927 their fourth child, Therese, was born. After Connie was hospitalised, Margaret returned home and went to school in Astoria. Connie then came home to die and Mary nursed him during his final days. He died on Tuesday 6 November 1928, which was election day in the United States.

Connie had been much too ill to vote, but he had insisted that Mary go out and do so, as it had been a particularly controversial campaign. The Democratic Party candidate, Al Smith, was the first Roman Catholic to be nominated by a major party for the presidency. This unleashed a tremendous wave of anti-Catholicism. Some people in Protestant America were terrified that the Pope would take over the White House if Smith was elected. Opponents openly contended that 'A vote for Al Smith is a vote for the Pope.' There was never much chance of any Democrat winning that election, because the country was in the midst of unprecedented prosperity. It was the 'Roaring Twenties', and Charlie Klenke's old boss, Herbert Hoover, was a virtual certainty to be elected.

In view of the circumstances of her father's death, Margaret never forgot the bitterness of that election campaign. 'This prejudice came out loud and clear,' she recalled. 'Al Smith did not even carry New York, where he had twice been elected governor.' Protestant friends suddenly became anti-Catholic. 'It was amazing the stupidity of people, thinking the Pope would come over to Washington to run the country.' Mary Harrigan became active in local politics in the following years as a staunch Democrat and she was employed by the party at election time. That paid better than nursing. In addition to the state and local campaigns, she worked for Franklin D. Roosevelt's presidential campaign in 1932 and again in 1936, but she lost respect for him when he sought an unprecedented third term. She supported his campaign manager, James A. Farley, for the Democratic nomination in 1940.

2

THE DEPRESSION YEARS

Shortly after Connie died, Mary Harrigan moved to
Sunnyside on Long Island with Margaret and Therese. It
was a stopping-off place for the upwardly mobile middle-
class and lower-middle-class families of those German,
Irish, Italian and Jewish emigrants who wished to escape
the city but could not afford the haven of real suburbia.
The Krauses had bought an eight-family house in Sunnyside and they had a vacant apartment, so the three
Harrigans moved into it. They were in the new apartment
for Christmas 1928. It was a pretty horrific Christmas,
because Mary had lost her husband and two daughters
within the space of less than two years, but Margaret never
forgot a gift from her godmother, Anna Sheehan. It was
the most beautiful dressing gown of panne velvet, lined
with pale-pink satin, and it had marabou around it. 'I
thought it was the most gorgeous thing I ever had and it
sort of brightened Christmas,' Margaret said.

At the time, the widow's pension was a meagre amount
that did not even cover their rent, so Mary had to go
back to working as a nurse. But this was at the onset of
the Great Depression, and work was scarce. She generally

worked as a temporary nurse at the local hospital or did private duty on occasions. Freda Krause also worked. Her mother-in-law would look after Therese during the day, if Mary and Freda were working. Then Margaret would come home from school and take over with Therese and prepare the food for the evening meal, until it was ready to cook. Mary would then cook it when she got home.

Throughout this period, an Irish friend of theirs, Margaret Furlong from County Wexford, helped out. She was a friend of Mary and Connie and was godmother to Therese. She worked as an attendant at the mental hospital on Ward's Island and was known to the Harrigan children as 'Aunt Margaret'. 'Money was very, very scarce during the depressions, and if it weren't for Aunt Margaret, I don't know what we would have done, because she gave Mother a lot of her salary – certainly over half of it,' Margaret recalled. The children of the neighbourhood played together, and Margaret remembered that they had a skating pond during the winter and there was one particularly bad snowstorm. Only doctors were allowed to use their cars on the dangerous roads. With the roads closed to most traffic, the children were able to go sledding down Stillman Avenue, which was a very steep hill.

Margaret and Billie Kraus were inseparable friends for as long as Margaret could remember. Billie was a little over a year older than her and the Krauses used to take Margaret with them when they drove out to Jones' Beach, which was much further out on Long Island. On the way they had to pass Idlewild, which was then a salt marsh. They would have to roll up the windows and hold their noses, because there was a foul smell from the marsh, which is now the site of John F. Kennedy Airport. Mary often took the children into New York City, and they would travel on the open bus down Fifth Avenue, go to Central Park and visit the zoo, or go to the movies. During the remainder of the year the movie matinées were a fairly regular treat on Saturdays, because serials were very popular at the time. These were the forerunners of the soap operas. Each episode usually ended on the brink of some kind of climax to entice the children to come again the following week to find out what happened. The movies were a treat in either good or bad weather, because during the winter the cinemas were warm and they were air-conditioned during the summer.

There were some terrible polio epidemics during the summer. When these struck, the cinemas and swimming pools were closed down. The children stayed in their own little groups and avoided crowds during the epidemics. At the time nobody knew how the dreaded disease was passed on. It was not a respecter of persons, young or old, rich or poor. One of those afflicted was Franklin D. Roosevelt, then governor of New York and shortly to become president of the United States. He had been restricted to a wheelchair after contracting polio. 'I remember an ambulance coming and taking a child away in Forty-ninth Street, and we all being so scared that we were going to develop polio,' Margaret recalled more than three quarters of a century later. 'But thank God, we never did, neither the Krauses nor us, nor any immediate friend that I ever knew. We were lucky people . . . On the whole it was a very happy childhood, even though it was a very frugal life.'

When Mary wasn't nursing, she would turn her hand

to making clothes. Freda Kraus would buy the material, and Mary would makes clothes for all the children out of it. Once Therese became old enough, Mary used to take a job during July and August at Camp Laurel in downstate New Jersey, so that the children could attend the summer camp, which was mainly for the children of well-to-do parents. Various activities were arranged for the children, such as swimming, horse riding, tennis and basketball, as well as hiking and similar outdoor activities. Mary worked as camp nurse, while Margaret worked as a waitress in 1933 and as a counsellor in 1934 and 1935. This covered all the children's expenses at the camp, and had the advantage of getting them out of the city, away from the fear of polio during the hot summer months. Margaret could not go to a Catholic school in Sunnyside, because the parochial school there finished at the fifth grade, and she was already in this grade, so she attended public school for the first time. 'It was like absolute heaven,' she recalled, 'because the nun I had left in Lady of Mount Carmel was a very sadistic woman. She had me scared stupid, and when you are scared stupid, you *are* stupid.' Her teacher in Public School 125 was a lovely man who treated his pupils like intelligent adults. Children just blossomed under him.

In the seventh grade, Margaret was moved into 'rapid-development class', which completed seventh and eighth grades in just one year. She was very good at history and geography, and good at English, but terrible at mathematics. 'How I passed it, I'll never know. It had to be Somebody above me, because it sure wasn't me,' she said. The students at the school had desks for two, and

Margaret shared her desk with Judith Tuvim for the two and a half years. Judy later became famous as an actress under the stage name of Judy Holliday. In 1951 she won the Oscar for Best Actress for her role as Billie Dawn, the blonde bimbo in the movie *Born Yesterday*. She also won a Tony for a similar role as Ella Peterson in the Broadway hit musical *Bells Are Ringing* in 1957. She had a brilliant stage and screen career but died tragically young, of cancer, in 1965. At school Judy was very much the opposite of the roles in which she became famous. 'She was a pretty and brilliant girl with a photographic memory,' according to Margaret. 'Oh God, she could look at the cover of a book and she had it all memorised. She was really a brilliant, brilliant girl. Of course, she wasn't a blonde then; she was small, with very dark curly hair. She was a Jewish girl, and very nice.' At the time, Judy's IQ was assessed at 172, well above the genius level of 140. She later changed her name for the stage because people were always getting it wrong, or mispronouncing it. Tuvim was the Hebrew for 'holy day', so she adopted the stage name 'Judy Holliday'.

In later life she did not talk much about her childhood, because she said that she could not remember much of it. Her parents divorced when she was just six years old. This clearly had a traumatic effect on her. When asked about those early years, she said she would always come up with a blank. 'You know what that means,' she explained. 'I guess it's pretty obvious that I was unhappy.' After her parents broke up, her grandmother lived with her and her mother, and she indoctrinated Judy in socialist and liberal ideas. Judy found an escape in reading books.

'I always loved words,' she said. 'I ate up all the books I could lay my hands on, and when I couldn't get books, I read candy wrappers and labels on cereal and toothpaste boxes.' In primary school, while the others in her class were reading children's books, she was reading the likes of Tolstoy's *War and Peace*, and the plays of Shakespeare. In her final year in the school she won a prize for her essay 'How to Keep the Streets, Parks and Playgrounds of Our City Clean and Wholesome'.

Judy shared Margaret's dislike of mathematics. 'I probably would never have passed geometry except that by mistake they gave the same test twice and I remembered the right answers,' Judy explained. 'I do have a good memory. I got a kick out of being different and improving myself and everyone around me. I must have been obnoxious.' That was never the way Margaret remembered her. She remembered Judy not only as an extremely intelligent person with a strong social conscience, but also as a very small individual. This was because Judy was two years younger than most of the girls in her class. Margaret never realised that Judy was so young, because in some ways she seemed very advanced. She seemed to know a tremendous amount about sex, and Margaret noted that she learned a lot from her. It seemed that the Jewish girls always knew more about sex than the rather repressed Catholic girls. There was another brilliant girl in the class, Gladys Kalmus, whose aunt and uncle started Technicolor and were known in Hollywood as 'the king and queen of Technicolor'. Margaret did not know what happened to Gladys later on, because she did not go to the same high school as her. She used to say that she was planning to join her uncle in Hollywood as soon as she finished school.

They had a graduation from Public School 125 in June 1932 and Margaret was thrilled with her first long evening frock. She then went to Newtown High School in Elmhurst. She joined the Newman Club, which was the Catholic organisation in public schools. Their chaplain was from St Sebastian Church. When they went to Confession to him, there might be one student on one side of him and another on the other side. He would ask the first pupil to wait and, after hearing the other's Confession, he would then open up the two slots and hold a conversation with the two pupils about the next basketball game or social event. Years later in Ireland, Margaret was surprised to find that people could not get out of the Confession boxes fast enough. They certainly did not stop for a chat with the priest, or acknowledge that they knew him. The chaplain was a great man for organizing and keeping young people together. It did not matter whether it was a roller-skating derby, or whatever the season indicated. Boys and girls did them all together.

In her final year of high school, Margaret dated a number of different boys. Her friends Frances and Kathleen Hanley were at college at the time, and through them she met one of their college friends, Eugene McNulty, with whom she had a number of dates. He later became famous as 'Dennis Day'. He made a name for himself as a singer on *The Jack Benny Show* and later had his own television show and starred in a number of movies. In her final-year school annual, the pen sketch beside Margaret's photograph declared: 'Lively, likeable, jolly withal. Ready to answer fun's first call.'

After Margaret's graduation from Newtown High School in June 1936, her mother decided to take the whole family on a holiday to Ireland. Mary had not been home since she emigrated in 1911, and this seemed an ideal time for a visit, twenty-five years later. She had planned to return in 1920 when her father was sick, but he recovered, and she could not make the trip in 1927 when her mother was dying, because she had had a baby that year and her own husband was dying. Her father, now blind, obviously would not have long to live, so she decided to see her father and to introduce Margaret to her roots before she set off into the world. It became the holiday of a lifetime. Mary was forty-eight years old, while Margaret was seventeen and Therese was just eight. They initially planned to sail on the SS *Manhattan*, which was bringing the main batch of the American team to the Berlin Olympics. Mary's first cousin Mimi Zimmerman (née Drummond) and her husband, Charlie, were travelling on the same boat, but Therese became ill with pneumonia and the Harrigans had to postpone their trip to the next sailing the following week. They went, instead, on the SS *President Harding*, another of the United States Lines' four liners which plied the North Atlantic.

The ship set sail from New York on 22 July with four ports of call: Cobh, Plymouth, Le Havre and Hamburg. The passengers included the second batch of members of the United States team bound for the Berlin Olympics. It included the rowers, competitors in the canoeing events, and some field-event athletes. After overcoming seasickness on the second day, Margaret had a terrific time. She first befriended a young man going by the name of Norman Johnston, but a couple of days later he was apprehended as a stowaway. 'Was I surprised!' Margaret noted in a diary at the time. The Olympic team invited her to join in volleyball games and their keep-fit sessions with a fifteen-pound medicine ball. Each morning she found herself very stiff from all the exercise. At night she was able to go the Barbary Coast Bar on board the ship and drink some Tom Collinses.

In the circumstances, the six-day trip to Cobh was all too short, and Margaret had a lump in her throat leaving the *President Harding*, even though she was impressed with her first view of Ireland bathed in sunshine. 'Ireland looks lovely,' she noted. She was later anxious to follow the exploits of the American Olympians, but there was very little coverage of the games on Irish radio. There had been a split in Irish athletics the previous year, and Ireland did not send a team to Berlin. Margaret did not learn until afterwards that the cox and eight of the men on the ship had won gold medals in the eights rowing event.

Since her father died, she had had very little contact with any relatives, other than Mimi Zimmerman. Margaret did have memories of her great-grand-aunt Mary Golden, who had lived near them in New York in the very early years. She was a sister of Mary's Grandmother McQuinn. In those days they were also in regular contact with the Harrigans. On arriving in Ireland, Margaret and Therese were introduced to a whole host of Irish cousins. They were met at the boat by Mary's sister Anne, and her husband, Con Kennedy, who was a local-government official in Tralee. They came out on the tender and greeted the Harrigans as they got off the ship at around 8.30 AM. Con had used his contacts to ensure that they were speedily processed by Customs, and Mary's brother, Tom Ryle, the stationmaster in Killorglin, had asked his railway contacts to facilitate them on the train journey to Tralee. It was an arduous train trip on old-fashioned steam trains. They had to change trains at both Cork and Mallow. At around 4.30 PM, the train finally arrived in Tralee, where they were met by members of several different families of relatives: the O'Connors, the Kennedys, the Drummonds and the Ryles.

They stayed at the home of Mary's sister Kitty O'Connor, a small semi-detached three-bedroom house in Castle Countess. It must have been a squeeze, with the five O'Connors and the three Harrigans staying there. But then, this was the time of the extended family, when people made do with much less. 'Everything was so new here and there was so many things to do and see,' Margaret wrote in a travel diary. On their first full day in Ireland, the sun was shining, so they went out to Banna beach, with fourteen of them packed into an ordinary saloon car. The crowd of children were squashed in, on the floor, and sitting in each other's laps. It seemed to Margaret that the cars in Ireland never went anywhere with just one or two people, because that would have been a waste of petrol. 'We had a swim,' she noted, 'but it was very cold, so we did not stay in long.' She never did get used to the much colder sea water in Ireland. That night they went to the movies and Margaret was stunned to find it was still daylight following the late movie. Even on the longest days in New York, it had never been bright much later than eight o'clock in the evening.

The first week was a long round of visiting various relatives. Mimi and Charlie Zimmermann came to visit them on a donkey and cart, borrowed from Joanie O'Connell in Upper Rock Street – much to the disgust of all the aunts, who thought that only some crazy returned Yank would wish to be seen on a donkey and cart. 'Mother, Aunt Gerty and Aunt Kitty were horrified,' Margaret noted. They wondered what the neighbours would think. 'My God, she is doing the typical Yank!' one of them exclaimed. To make things worse, somebody took pictures of them with Margaret and Therese on the donkey and cart. 'God Almighty, what's wrong with Mimi Drummond? Of course, she was always giddy!' Gerty said, answering her own question.

The weather turned poor and Margaret suddenly discovered that there was not very much to do in bad weather. 'You can't seem to do anything here because of the awful weather,' she wrote on 3 August. The movies seemed to be the only escape. 'Still cloudy,' she wrote two days later. 'It doesn't seem as if it will ever clear.' The big news in town that week was that a strike that had lasted sixteen weeks against the large merchant traders in town had ended. On 9 August the family went to Killorglin by train to visit Mary's brother Tom and to go to Puck Fair. 'The scenery was very beautiful all the way out,' Margaret wrote. That night she went downtown with her uncle and family. 'We saw Puck raised,' she recalled. (Puck Fair, which dates back to before the advent of Christianity, involves crowning a goat king for three days and raising him on a high platform in the centre of Killorglin.)

The following week the weather turned for the better and they went for a drive around the Dingle Peninsula. They had dinner in Benner's Hotel in Dingle and then set off sightseeing around Slea Head. 'The scenery was the most beautiful I have ever seen, beyond all description,' Margaret noted in her diary. 'We saw the Blasket Islands very clearly, and we met some of the islanders – very nice people, speak only Irish. Out west in 1936 the only people that spoke English, if you were looking for directions or anything, were kids who were in school, because they learned English in school.' The young children and the older people spoke only Irish. The area was really a Gaeltacht at that time. On the way home they had tea in Dingle and returned to Tralee via the Connor Pass, which she described as 'very cloudy but beautiful'.

The next day they went to Killarney to visit one of Mary's aunts, and they went sightseeing there. That evening they had tea at the International Hotel. Margaret was amazed at the crossroads dancing on fine summer evenings in Ballyard, on the south side of Tralee. There was a platform up at the top of Ballyard, and there would be musicians there with a fiddle and a melodeon for the dancing. 'It made you very light on your feet,' she noted. The bitterness of the Black-and-Tan period was still noticeable in 1936. Indeed, the Economic War with Britain was on at the time and some people frowned on all things British. The kind of dancing that young people were doing in the United States and Britain was frequently denounced as 'English dancing'. During her stay, Margaret was taken by car to dances in Killarney and

Ballybunion. She had the time of her life and did not want to return to America when the time came. 'I didn't want to go back to the States,' she recalled. 'No way. I certainly cried copious tears leaving Ireland. I loved it here. I had a great time. I met lovely, lovely people.' But Con Kennedy persuaded her that she should go back and take a secretarial course so that she could come back to Ireland and get a job.

The Harrigans left Tralee on 3 October to return to the United States on the MV *Britannic*. They spent the night at the Westbowline Hotel in Cobh, along with Mary's sister Kitty and her husband, Michael O'Connor. They came out on the tender with the travellers in the early morning. They sighted the liner at about eight o'clock. It was a massive ship owned by the White Star Cunard Line. It had been called after a sister ship of the *Titanic* that had been sunk during the First World War. Once they boarded the ship, there was little to do. 'The sea was rather bad, so we went to sleep in our cabin,' Margaret noted. Next day was spent trying to get their sea legs. The second day was Margaret's birthday. 'Am eighteen today with a birthday in the middle of the Atlantic,' she wrote.

3

WORKING AT AT&T

After returning from the holiday in Ireland, Margaret went to secretarial school for a while but then quit when she got a job as a telephone operator with AT&T in New York in early 1937. America was only slowly emerging from the Great Depression. Things were still difficult in the Harrigan household. Margaret gave her mother her weekly salary and kept only what she could make by doing overtime.

One of the more interesting aspects of being a operator was listening to the conversations of different celebrities, especially during quiet periods while on night duty. One operator might just call out to 'Listen to LA 4' and, if they were not busy, as many as twenty-five operators might then listen in to the conversation on that line. By pulling the switch backwards, they could listen in undetected. When the switch was upright, the operator could not hear the people on the line, and the operator pushed the switch forwards to open the line in order to speak to the person on the line.

Operators were particularly interested in entertainment celebrities, and they were often privy to shocking conversations, such as ones referring to the fact that singers Nelson Eddy and Al Jolson contracted syphilis from a particular actress in Hollywood. Jolson was an international celebrity not only because of his singing but also because he had starred in the first talking movie, *The Jazz Singer*, in 1927. He married Ruby Keeler, a Canadian-born dancer who made it big on Broadway before going to Hollywood, where she met Jolson. She retired from show business during their marriage, which lasted for over a decade but came to a sticky end when she learned that Jolson had not only contracted syphilis through his philandering but, worse, had passed it on to her. Margaret heard their telephone conversation after Ruby learned that she had syphilis, which had until recently been a terminal disease. Jolson was sobbing as he pleaded with his wife to save their marriage, but she was in such a rage that she was implacable.

Vivien Leigh was on the way towards becoming probably the world's most famous actresses at the time, as a result of her starring role in *Gone With the Wind*. She was having a torrid affair with Laurence Olivier, even though both of them were married to other people. The affair was one of the worst-kept secrets in Hollywood. It was the subject of the kind of gossip that later surrounded the affair between Richard Burton and Liz Taylor before they got married in the 1960s. The telephone conversations between Leigh and Olivier were of a particularly shocking variety, as they were very sexually explicit. They called each other by pet names. She called him 'Baba', and he called her 'Pussy'. Olivier was a consummate actor and he was probably acting not only for Leigh, but also for the operators. 'How do you know when Larry is acting and when he is not?' one of his wives was once asked. 'Oh,' she replied, 'he's acting all the time.' Vivien, on the other hand, was one of those outspoken women who had an overactive sense of the dramatic. She never cared who heard her. 'You wouldn't hear if you closed the door,' was her attitude. She and Olivier divorced their spouses and subsequently married, but that, too, ended in divorce.

Sunday 30 October 1938 was Halloween, and Margaret was working that evening. At eight o'clock the Columbia Broadcasting System was broadcasting *Mercury Theatre on the Air,* which had been going on for the previous four months. That night the one-hour programme was an adaptation for radio of *War of the Worlds* by H. G. Wells. The programme took the form of a documentary. Following the normal introduction, dance music, supposedly coming from the Meridian Room in the Park Plaza Hotel in New York City, was broadcast. This was then interrupted by a series of newsflashes from different parts of the country. A professor at a Chicago observatory reported a series of explosions on Mars. The programme returned to the dance music.

Shortly afterwards there was another interruption; this time it was an interview with a professor of the National History Museum in New York. He reported that something had hit the Earth near Princeton, New Jersey, and he suggested that it might have had 'something to do with the disturbances' on Mars. After another brief spell of music, there was a report from a farm at Grovers Mill, New Jersey, where a strange object had landed. This was followed by a description of a huge creature with tentacles crawling out of the object, then, shortly afterwards, by a report that at least forty people had been killed at Grovers Mill. People who tuned in to the programme after the start did not realise that this was just a dramatisation of a book. They thought it was a breaking news story, even though all the other networks continued with their regular programmes. Then there was a report that the first of the creatures had reached New York City.

Margaret and her colleagues got thousands of calls, as operators from around the country tried to find out what was happening in New York. 'Are you all right, New York?' they kept asking. 'What is happening there?' It was against company policy to chat to other operators, other than about business matters, but this was a most unusual occasion. The callers disclosed that there were reports that Martians had landed in New Jersey and that New York was under attack. They wanted to know what the Martians looked like. Some of the operators went to the windows and reported back that everything looked normal. '*War of the Worlds* has no further significance than as the holiday offering it was intended to be,' Orson Welles announced at the end of the programme. 'The Mercury Theatre's own radio version of dressing up in a sheet and jumping out of a bush and saying "Boo!" . . . So goodbye everybody, and remember please for the next day or so the terrible lesson you learned tonight. That grinning, glowing, globular invader of your living room is an inhabitant of the pumpkin patch, and if your doorbell rings and nobody's there, that was no Martian; it's Halloween.'

In January 1939, Margaret went on the road as part of

an effort to personalise the telephone service instigated by AT&T. There were three teams of six demonstrators who toured the country showing other operators how to handle different situations. At twenty, Margaret was the youngest of the demonstrators. She had to have her mother's formal permission to travel. The team consisted of five women and one man. Company regulations stipulated that only men could fly; the women had to travel by train. 'Don't ask me the logic of that,' she said. Of course, this was the heyday of long-distance rail travel. The trains had fancy club cars and Pullman sleeping quarters, and while travelling for the company, AT&T employees stayed in the best hotels.

Margaret's first venture was to Cleveland, Ohio. She set out with the others from New York at 8 PM on 8 January. They arrived at their destination at 7.30 the following morning. They rehearsed their demonstration during the day and went to the movies that night. Next day they gave their first demonstration in the afternoon and another one that evening. They were entertained to dinner by the local staff of AT&T. The following day they moved on to Detroit, where they were booked into the Statler Hotel. Throughout their travels, Margaret roomed with Mary Burns, the oldest member of the travelling team. She was a married woman. They went through the same routine on the first full day there: examining the facilities for their demonstration and practising. Then four of them went out on the town together. 'We started in the Wonder Bar and drank our supper,' Margaret noted. 'There was a floor show there and then we called at Davey Holshouser in Cin, and did we have fun! We left there about 8.30, then we skipped over to the Book Cadillac and decided it was too dead. We took a taxi over to the Cork Town Tavern. Gee, it was swell. We left there and took a taxi to the Bowery, which is two towns away. What a place, but what fun. Then a taxi back to the Statler.' After three demonstrations the next day, they moved on to Chicago. This was a very significant experience for a girl who was working away from home for the first time in her life.

Margaret's eleven-year-old sister, Therese, wrote from home. 'While you are away, Aunt Margaret will not let the dog in the living room,' Therese said. 'If Buttons even looks in there, she says, "Don't come in here", and Buts thinks she is calling her and, of course, she comes in and then there is war. Aunt Margaret is yelling at the dog. Please come home soon. If you don't, the dog will be dead, and does she miss you. When you say, "Where is Margaret?", she looks all around.'

After Chicago, the team returned to New York. Kathleen Hanley, who was by this time married to a man named Jules Coelos, invited Margaret to dinner at their home to hear about her travels on 23 January 1939. John G. Dwyer, an old friend, just happened to telephone her that afternoon, and she invited him to dinner too. John, who was a chemist working in New Jersey, never forgot meeting Margaret that evening. He always maintained that it was love at first sight, but it was obviously different for Margaret. She already had a boyfriend. Margaret was back on the road the following month. They left New York for Missouri on the afternoon of Saturday 11 February 1939 on *The Spirit of St Louis*, a train named after the famous plane flown by Charles Lindbergh.

They did not get to St Louis until shortly after noon the following Monday. 'We got our first glance at the new oil wells,' she noted. 'Then came the Mississippi river – rather disappointing.' They had luxurious facilities at the Hotel Coranado. 'Mary and I had an apartment consisting of a foyer, living room, dressing room, bathroom, dining room and kitchen,' Margaret wrote. 'It was perfect.' It was significant that she did not mention the bedroom, but then they were so tired by the time they got to bed that they probably hardly noticed their surroundings.

Her diary account of her whirlwind eight-day trip to Missouri and back provides a flavour of the lifestyle that the young women enjoyed while personalising the service of AT&T. They had four demonstrations the day after travelling to St Louis. After dinner and a drink at the hotel, they retired early, as they were tired. There were four more demonstrations the following day. They had dinner at the Hotel Jefferson, then went to the Hotel Claridge for drinks, back to their own hotel and out to the Hotel Roosevelt, where they danced. They then went to the Plantation Club, where the novelty was black entertainers. 'The floor show did not come on until 3 AM, and of course we waited,' Margaret wrote. They did not get back to the hotel until 4.30 AM. The next morning, one of the men took them on a sightseeing tour of St Louis, and they took an afternoon train to Kansas City. The train trip was particularly memorable because the train had the latest-model engine, and travelled at a hundred miles an hour. The accommodation in Kansas

City was not as luxurious as it had been in St Louis, but they did have an unforgettable meal at the Green Parrot, a restaurant on a hill overlooking the city. 'When you go in the door, you step into the living room and then into the dining room,' Margaret wrote. 'The waitresses are dressed in flowered uniforms. The meal was great. We had a platter of southern-fried chicken and corn, sweet potatoes, Spanish rice, string beans, cottage cheese and preserved apples.' Sixty years later, she would still remember that as one of the best restaurants and best meals she had ever had. After three more demonstrations the following day, they were taken to a Southern mansion for dinner. 'The place was beautiful and we had a grand time,' she said. They danced and then went back for a late-evening demonstration. 'After that, we went to Old Heidelberg and had fun.'

The next morning they took an early train back to St Louis, where they caught *The Spirit of St Louis* for New York. A new club car had been added to the train and they enjoyed the trip home, arriving back in New York on Sunday afternoon. In the following weeks, Margaret took a holiday in Miami and then went to Boston in April. Other trips took her to Denver, Colorado, and San Francisco. On the Sunday that Britain and France declared war on Germany, Mary Harrigan was at home with Therese, who remembered that her mother became upset. 'What is going to happen to Ireland?' she cried. Therese, who had recently had her twelfth birthday, never forgot that moment. She did not realise that her mother was really thinking of her friends and relations – the people she knew in Ireland. Therese thought her mother was worried about the country, and she could not understand it. No matter what happened in the war, the island would still be there, she reasoned. Those born in America were not that concerned, because Europe was so far away and America had an avowed policy of isolation. That afternoon Margaret went out to the home of family friends in Breezy Point, New York, and was listening to a baseball game on the radio. An announcer interrupted the game a number of times with news from Europe. The war seemed so far away that America was insulated from it. They had no idea that day what fate had in store. Those trying to listen to the baseball game between the New York Giants and the Brooklyn Dodgers were more than a little irritated at the interruptions. 'Don't they realise the importance of the game?' someone asked. On the other side of the Atlantic, people in Ireland were more interested in the all-Ireland hurling final at Croke Park between Kilkenny and Cork. It was a cracker of a game that was remembered as the thunder-and-lighting final because it ended in a heavy thunderstorm with lashing rain, as Kilkenny held out to win by a single point.

With the war on in Europe, Margaret was transferred to become an overseas operator. This entailed putting through calls to and from the United States by radio telephone. Reception was frequently bad due to sunspots, and this made life particularly interesting. Sometimes they would have to get an engineer to try to improve the reception. Margaret remembered one night when they were having particular trouble with calls from the Canary Islands. The engineer had to speak up to be heard on the other end. He was trying to get the operator or engineer in the Canary Islands to talk so that he could get a voice-level. 'Have you many canaries there?' he asked. The person at the other end explained that the name was a misnomer, because there were no canaries native to the islands. Other similar famous misnomers would be 'Iceland' and 'Greenland', but the engineer surprised all the operators in New York with his response. 'Oh, I understand,' he said. 'It's like the Virgin Islands!'

In addition to putting through telephone calls, Margaret used to broadcast a regular shipping forecast. That was a bit of a curse because there was so many strange place names, and there was a man on Staten Island who used to call to complain about any mispronunciation. If AT&T did not placate him, he would complain to the Federal Communications Commission, and this inevitably upset the powers at AT&T. The man on Staten Island was 'a right pain' as far as Margaret was concerned.

America stayed out of overt involvement in the war for over two years, but President Franklin D. Roosevelt never hid his strong sympathy for the Allies, though he did promise to keep the United States out of the conflict. An important relationship quickly developed between Roosevelt and Winston Churchill. During the First World War the two men had served in similar government posts. Roosevelt was Secretary of the Navy in Washington and Churchill was First Lord of the Admiralty in London. Churchill was reappointed to the same post at the start of the war in 1939. He had been in office barely a week when Roosevelt wrote to him. 'It is because you and I occupied similar positions in the World War that I want

you to know how glad I am that you are back in the Admiralty,' the president began. 'What I want you and the prime minister to know is that I shall at all times welcome it if you would keep me in touch personally with anything you want me to know about.' This letter did not reach London until 3 October.

Churchill obtained the approval of Prime Minister Neville Chamberlain and Lord Halifax, the foreign secretary, before responding, with a telephone call. The White House had alerted the British that the US naval attaché in Berlin had received a warning from Admiral Eric Reader of the German navy: German intelligence had learned that the American merchant ship *Iroquois* was going to be sunk in the Atlantic, presumably by the British – in an attempt to blame the Germans and thereby inflame American opinion in order to bring the United States into the war. The *Iroquois* was already about a thousand miles west of Ireland, and Churchill telephoned Roosevelt on 5 October to suggest that the main threat to a ship that far out into the Atlantic would be if a time bomb had been planted on the vessel during a stopover in Cobh. 'We think this not impossible,' he explained. Therefore he suggested that Roosevelt should urgently expose the full facts, especially his source of the information, in order to frustrate the plot. He also suggested that the crew of the *Iroquois* should be warned to search the ship, if this had not been done already. In his three-volume collection of the Roosevelt–Churchill correspondence, which included 1,688 messages of various kinds, the transcript of that telephone call was 'the only firm evidence' that William F. Kimball could find of any telephone conversations, although, he noted, 'There are suggestions that other calls took place during the early stage of their relationship.'

Margaret Harrigan put a number of these calls through both before Churchill became prime minister and in the period after May 1940, when he took over from Neville Chamberlain at 10 Downing Street. The calls were particularly memorable because the British and American operators engaged in a kind of game with each other. Each side tried to have the other's leader on the line first. If Churchill was calling, however, the American operators insisted that Churchill be on the line before they put the call through to the White House. Margaret explained that she would call the White House to learn whether President Roosevelt was available to take a call from Churchill. Once told that he was available, she would insist that Churchill be on the line before she called the White House again. On the other side, the British usually made a similar demand when Roosevelt initiated the call. The operators had to listen in to all calls as part of their job. They had to time the call and had to give credit for every time anyone had to repeat something due to the quality of the connection. There was no privacy on those lines – anybody with a short-wave radio could listen in if they had the correct frequency. Roosevelt and Churchill knew this, so they talked in a very general way about the matter in hand. Only someone who was privy to their correspondence and previous discussions would realise what they were talking about. In the circumstances, Margaret did not remember any specifics of their conversations.

News of the Japanese attack on Pearl Harbour broke on the afternoon of Sunday 7 December 1941. Everyone who was old enough remembered where they were when they heard the news of the attack. Margaret was at home with a boyfriend, Don Hudson, when her mother turned on the radio, which was giving news of the attack. 'The fools,' her mother said indignantly. 'Orson Welles is doing it again!' But then Margaret received a call from AT&T, telling her that all operators were being called to work immediately, as Pearl Harbour had been attacked. America was at war.

For some time previously there had been a lot of construction activity in a room behind where the overseas operators were working. None of the operators knew what was happening there, but it now quickly became apparent that it was an intelligence operation. Navy intelligence had been preparing to take control of overseas calls once the United States entered the war. As of 1941, many people realised that it was not a question of *if* but of *when* America would enter the conflict. For instance, David Gray, the American ambassador in Dublin, had been telling the Irish government for over a year that it was only a matter of time before the United States would go to war. This was not official government policy, but Gray – who was married to an aunt of First Lady Eleanor Roosevelt – had Roosevelt's personal approval and full blessing to say what he had been predicting. Navy intelligence took control of the overseas operations of AT&T, and all operators of German, Italian or Japanese ancestry were transferred to other duties, as were those of Swiss extraction. For some reason, Irish-Americans were not affected, even though Ireland officially remained neutral throughout the war.

With the transfer of so many operators, the overseas

operations of AT&T were suddenly short-staffed, and it would be two days before Margaret would get home again. The navy censors did allow some calls through, but most callers were simply told that their call could not be put through and were given no explanation. Margaret Harrigan was only aware of one call ever being put through to Ireland during the war. This was because there was a secret arrangement with the British for all overseas calls from Ireland to be routed through London for security reasons. This was a means of assuring the British that the Irish were doing everything they could to ensure that Irish territory was not being used to help the Axis in any way or to hinder British war efforts. The British did leave a telegraph line open for the German ambassador to contact Berne, Switzerland, as a kind of quid pro quo for the Germans leaving the line open from London. The German minister to Ireland, Edouard Hempel, used the telegraph line to send his reports to Berlin, via Berne, but unknown to him, the British had broken his code, so they were reading his messages before they even got to their destination.

The British did not allow any transatlantic calls to be patched through to Dublin. But in the final week of December 1941, they put through a call from the film star Maureen O'Hara – much to Margaret's surprise. This was around the time of Maureen O'Hara's wedding to the movie director William Price. Born Maureen Fitzsimons in Ranelagh, Dublin, she was the second of six children of Charles and Marguerite Fitzsimons. Her father was a clothier in Dublin and part-owner of Shamrock Rovers soccer team, while her mother operated a chic

couture salon adjacent to the Shelbourne Hotel. Although only twenty-one years old, Maureen was already a recognised movie star. In 1938 she had come to the attention of Charles Laughton, who gave her a starring role, under the stage name 'Maureen O'Hara', in his film *Jamaica Inn*. The following year she got married, but her family whisked her off to Hollywood before the marriage was consummated, so it was annulled. In 1941, she starred in John Ford's *How Green Was My Valley*, which turned out to be a sensation that would win six Academy Awards. Maureen went on to have probably the most distinguished movie career of any Irish-born actress, playing opposite some of the most successful screen stars of her generation: Tyrone Power, Douglas Fairbanks Jr, Errol Flynn, Henry Fonda, James Stewart, Alec Guinness, Noel Coward, Rex Harrison, Ralph Richardson and John Wayne. Due to her own mother's Irish connections, Margaret Harrigan remembers putting through Maureen O'Hara's call. During that call, Maureen explained that her new husband had arranged the call thanks to the influence of his friend Sumner Welles, the Under-Secretary of State in Washington.

Roosevelt and Churchill continued to telephone each other after America entered the war, but now, once their calls were set up, scramblers were used on both ends. The conversation then became unintelligible to the operators, who had to take an oath of secrecy in relation to their work, and they were told that their home telephones would be tapped to ensure their loyalty. The American navy had suffered terrible destruction at Pearl Harbour, where over three thousand American servicemen were killed. This was followed by a whole series of American setbacks in the Pacific. Overseas telephone operators were quickly introduced to the kind of harrowing insights to which they would become privy when the American forces were overrun in the Philippines. The surrender at Bataan in April 1942 was, at the time, the biggest surrender ever of American forces abroad. This was followed on 6 May by the surrender at nearby Corregidor.

For twenty-four hours, all the available operators scribbled down messages from the men in the Philippines for their loved ones at home. Normally operators in San Francisco would have passed on calls only for the eastern half of the country to New York, but there were so many calls and time was so short that San Francisco did not have time to screen them. About half of the calls were just patched through to New York, where operators took messages for people, even if they were living on the West Coast. They put the men on speakers as operators furiously scribbled down their particular messages. There was no time to put the men through to their families. 'They all gave us their names and they asked us to call their parents and wives to say they were all right, they were surrendering,' Margaret told journalist Breda Joy during a 1998 interview. Margaret's voice was breaking. 'So many of them didn't get back. That was a tragic day. As you can see, it still . . . ' she choked up, her eyes filling with tears. 'They were all young. We were all young. Then a Japanese person came on at the other end and shouted in English, "Death to all Americans!" This was followed by an eerie radio silence.' Operators then had the harrowing duty of passing on the messages to the families of the men. Of course, people did not realise at the time that the soldiers who surrendered would be subjected to inhuman treatment in the Japanese prisoner-of-war camps. The Japanese despised anyone who surrendered: they felt that people were honour-bound to commit suicide first. Hence they treated the prisoners taken at Bataan and Corregidor with utter contempt. Many died as a result of the brutal treatment they received.

On one occasion, Margaret had put through a call from a US army general in Cuba. The general mentioned something about the weather and the intelligence officer instructed Margaret to tell him that he could not speak about the weather. The call could be overheard very easily and weather information was considered of strategic military importance. The general resented being told that he could not speak about the weather. He was not going to be told what he could and could not do by some operator. When he persisted in talking about the weather, the censor just cut him off. Shortly afterwards, the navy intelligence officer was ordered to report to his head-quarters immediately. He left, taking the record of the conversation with him. Not long afterwards, he returned to duty looking distinctly content, satisfied that one arrogant general was now in the soup.

The most harrowing calls that Margaret transmitted were in August 1942. She kept those to herself for over forty years. They were calls about the famous Allied landing at Dieppe on 17 August 1942. This was a raid involving some five thousand Allied soldiers, who were attempting to seize the town of Dieppe in France. The Germans were forewarned of an impending attack on the

French coast, so they were prepared. Lord Louis Mount-batten planned the operation. There is still confusion as to its actual purpose. In part it was just a gesture to placate Joseph Stalin and the Soviets, who were calling on the Allies to set up a second front in Europe. Around four thousand Canadian troops took part, along with around one thousand British and about five hundred American soldiers. It was a disaster. High cliffs surrounded the beaches, and most of the men never managed to get off the beaches.

Margaret had to listen in to senior officers as they explained that they were receiving distress calls from the men on the beaches at Dieppe, who said they were being cut to pieces. They were calling for back-up, but there was little that the government could do at that stage. From what they said, Margaret and the other operators on duty that day thought that this was the D-Day invasion of Europe and that the whole thing had gone horribly wrong. Haunted by what had been said on those trans-atlantic calls, she thought the Allies were covering up a monumental military disaster. She could not discuss this with anyone, as she was sworn to secrecy. All the operators were disturbed about it for days. At home, Margaret's mother kept asking her what was wrong. Her mother might well have thought at the time that Margaret was upset about her love life, but that is another story: at the time, she had three different men trying to marry her. 'My mother was ready to kill me,' she told Breda Joy in a 1998 interview. 'I never meant to. It just happened. It was that time of life. They all got the idea I was going to marry them, and I wasn't.'

4

LOVE AT FIRST SIGHT

Johnny Dwyer never forgot the 'cold and very windy night' in January 1939 when he first met Margaret Harrigan – in Brooklyn, at the home of Kathleen Hanley Coeles. Although it was love at first sight for Johnny, he moved very slowly, as he was afraid she might think he was too keen or frivolous. He had very dark brown hair and a distinct five-o'clock shadow, as he had not shaved before the meeting, and he was worried that she would be turned off by his looks. She impressed him with her apparent self-sufficiency as she talked about her travels: she had already visited Ireland, Miami and Cleveland.

Johnny was born in Valparaíso, Chile, on 23 February 1916. His father, John A. (Jack) Dwyer, was working in Chile for Bethlehem Steel and he was also the US consul at Coquimbo, Chile. Both Johnny's father and his mother, Helen McGinley Dwyer, were born and reared in the United States. They returned there in 1919, along with Johnny and his younger brother, Owen, on what was supposed to be a holiday.

Jack and Helen both caught the Spanish influenza that ravaged the world that year. In the era before antibiotics,

61

influenza was often a lethal disease, and the Spanish flu was particularly dangerous for pregnant women. Helen was pregnant with a third child at the time and she died of the flu. Jack had to call off his plans to return to Chile. His mother in Bethlehem, Pennsylvania, looked after the two boys while they were in primary school. Jack married again, but his second wife, Kitty, did not want to be encumbered with children until she had children of her own. As a result, Johnny, who was very attached to his father, grew up with a distinct sense of grievance against his stepmother, even though it seems that he usually hid it. For a time, Owen was reared by a maternal aunt in Carteret, New Jersey, but then he moved to Rockville Centre to live with his father and a second growing family of two half-brothers and two half-sisters: Aurelie, Greg, Dorothy and Joe. Although Johnny developed a great affection for his half-brothers and half-sisters, he insisted on remaining with his grandmother and two maiden aunts. He finished high school in Bethlehem and went on to college at nearby Lehigh University, from which he graduated with a Bachelor of Science degree in chemistry on 6 October 1937.

After graduating, Johnny went to work on the quality-control side of the manufacture of cooking oil, first with the Southern Cotton Oil Company and later with the National Oil Products Company (Napco) of Harrison, New Jersey. America had still not fully emerged from the Great Depression. Even though Johnny was a college graduate, his earnings in 1937 came to $1,400, and the following year, when he changed jobs, they dropped slightly, to $1,261. While at university, he joined the

National Guard, and this did not help his employment prospects. 'Napco paid my helper twenty dollars more than me 'cause he was crippled and wouldn't be drafted,' he complained.

With the approach of war, Johnny seriously considered joining the regular army. On the night he first met Margaret Harrigan, he escorted her home. 'On the way home on the trolley, you asked me how come I didn't go ahead and get into the army like I wanted to,' he recalled three years later. 'You seemed to be so self-sufficient and able – with your stories about your travels. And then I met your mother and had a grand Irish cup of tea and a long chat with you. Then in February I got real brave and sent you a Valentine. Kathleen (at my question) told me that by all means I should ask you for a date. At that time I was recovering from a broken heart, the loss of a good job and a thin purse, so I didn't feel that I could let my ardour take too tangible form. You were my dream-girl anyway.'

'He was a gorgeous guy,' Margaret later explained. 'He was very good-looking, but it wasn't even that – he was really a wonderful person.'

The relationship developed slowly. On 8 July 1940 Johnny Dwyer was ordered to report for army duty with his National Guard unit. 'Napco tried to claim I was "indispensable to production efficiency" – which I told the army was not 100 per cent true,' he wrote. He was called up, supposedly for a year, but the following year his period of service was extended. Normally people do not have a detailed written account of the development of a relationship, because it develops in person, or at least over the telephone in more recent years. But during the upset of the Second World War, much of this relationship developed by mail. Margaret kept Johnny's letters, which frequently ran to six pages. 'I wish I had one of those all-wave radios with me,' he wrote from Fort Bragg, North Carolina, on 26 September 1941. 'Then I could listen in to the marine report (whatever it's about) and hear the voice of my colleen from Brooklyn. That would make this life a little more pleasant.'

While based in North Carolina, he wrote to Margaret every couple of weeks. These letters were usually about army life, or developments in New York, such as the performance of the Brooklyn Dodgers baseball team in the World Series. 'Ain't those Dodgers wonderful? Three to two today in their favor,' he wrote from a camp near Wedesborough, North Carolina, a couple of weeks later. 'I was thrilled to little bits when the boys all came out of the First Sergeant's tent cheering for "dem bums" at the end of the game.' As a Yank in the Deep South, he was obviously relieved at the news that he was about to be moved back to Fort Dix, New Jersey, in December 1941. 'This is without question God's country,' he wrote just before leaving North Carolina. 'Only He could love it.' While based at Fort Dix, New Jersey, he was able to met Margaret, but he was moved back south again the following month – this time to Camp Claiborne, Louisiana. From there, he wrote to Margaret on 26 January 1942. He began by quoting from a poem:

Margaret's great-grandparents Tadg McQuinn and Catherine Counihan McQuinn, who lived through the Famine but never talked about it

Thomas Ryle and Hanora McQuinn on their wedding day in 1887

The Ryle family, 1911. Back row, from left: Nora (Mother Bernard), Tom, Tommy and Kitty (O'Connor). Middle: Nance (Frazer), Hanora and Mary (Harrigan). Front: Anne (Kennedy) and Gerty (McLoughlin).

Mary Ryle and Cornelius Joseph Harrigan on
their wedding day, 2 September 1917

Margaret outside St Jean de
Baptiste Church, New York, in
a baby carriage that was used by
neighbours to bootleg alcohol
during Prohibition

Mary and Margaret, 1919

Margaret with her grandmother
Hannah (O'Sullivan) Harrigan,
a native of Cork city

Margaret (right) with her
sister Therese and their
mother, 1930

Mimi Drummond and her husband, Charlie Zimmerman,
with Therese and Margaret in Tralee, 1936

Margaret (back row, right) with her Irish cousins the
Drummonds, the Kennedys and the O'Connors in
Ballyheigue, 1936

The Dwyer family: Back row, left to right: Owen and John;
middle: Aurelie, Charles Gregory and Dorothy;
front: Kitty, Joe and Jack.

John Dwyer at Lehigh University,
spring 1937

In Newark, New Jersey,
August 1940

The Harrigan ladies
Therese (left), Margaret
(right) and their mother
in 1939

Margaret in Rockaway, New
York, on 3 September 1939,
the day Britain and France
declared war on Germany

Demonstrating for AT&T: Margaret is on the right, standing

The party held for Margaret in 1943 when she left AT&T to go and live in Georgia with Johnny. Margaret is fourth from left, front row.

Margaret and Johnny on their wedding day, 21 September 1942, with witnesses Captain Paul Moloney (left) and Major John Keider (right) outside Seattle Cathedral

The happy couple

Since last we parted with certain plan
Of future meeting or of an hour
To count a finite point within the span
Of endless time I find there is now power
That long can hold my mind bring surcease
From constant wondering what you think or do
In no preoccupation lies release
From circling thoughts and dreams of you
Since all of time is only pallid space
Between your leaving and your coming back
My mind projects the image of your face
Before my eyes as if to fill the lack
And still deceive with lingering hope.
Though late the hour and more the days, I wait – and wait.

'The thought and content of it expresses my feelings,' he wrote. 'I collected the quotation six years ago, and saved it for a time like this.' This was really the first written indication of the intensity of his feelings. 'January 23 was the anniversary of a cold windy night on Beverly Road in Brooklyn when I met the sweetest girl I know – and I mean you. (Gradually I'll work up to sending you my love. I'm sort of smuggling it along now.)' This was the first time he used the word 'love' in any of this letters.

Margaret's response to that letter is the earliest of her letters to survive. It was written in green ink. 'The ink is Therese's idea,' she wrote. 'She was sent for blue but decided our name wasn't Irish enough and we would have to prove our nationality by using green ink.' In this letter, Margaret mentioned that she was due ten days' holidays at the end of March or early April. 'I should love to come down and visit you for a few days,' she wrote. They talked on the telephone on 23 February, which happened to be Johnny's twenty-sixth birthday. They had known each other for three years, but neither knew the other's birthday. He did not say that it was his birthday but he mentioned in his next letter that he did not know hers. 'My birthday is October 6,' she replied. 'I was twenty-three on my last birthday.' She added that she was overcoming the flu. She had been working very hard in recent weeks, ever since the United States entered the war. She was obviously ill and was annoyed when her supervisor remarked that she 'should take better care' of herself. She blurted out that she had been working sixty to eighty hours a week.

Meeting Johnny in Louisiana proved impossible, because he was about to be moved to Sequim in the state of Washington, though he did not know where he was going at this time. Margaret did not mention anything in her letters about her work, but he obviously knew that she was privy to sensitive information. 'We don't know much about where we go from here – nothing, as a matter of fact,' he wrote on 25 March. 'I guess you know more about it that we do – through your telephone connections.' Johnny mentioned that he was glad to know Margaret's birthday. 'It's awful not to know such interesting items about people,' he continued. 'October 6 happens to be the anniversary of my graduation from Lehigh. That of course was a happy occasion – or at least it was a relief when the time arrived. My dad tells me he's had a few chats with you by phone, and he admonished me to write to you real soon. "She seems like a very nice girl.'" He signed off this letter with 'with l & x' but did not spell out the word 'love' or 'kisses'. The relationship was apparently taking off.

She sent him a mess kit with some sweets, as well as a pullover that she had knitted herself, and he responded by ordering an orchid to be delivered to her. 'You are positively the swellest girlfriend an unworthy soldier ever had,' he wrote on 6 April 1942. 'Both your Easter mess kit and the sweater reached me on Friday or Saturday before Easter, and you can be sure I was the happiest fellow west of Maine and east of Cape Flatter (Washington), and probably west of that too. The mess kit was perfect, and all the officers of the First Battalion 174th Combat Team thank you for the wine jellies you sent. They added a very fine touch to our mess. But they think the sweater you sent was meant for somebody else. Seems like it's about four inches above my belt.' 'She's been knitting it so long she forgot how you look,' his colleague Johnny Nolan remarked. 'What do I do now?' Johnny Dwyer asked Margaret. 'Maybe you can knit me a scarf for around my waist? It's the nicest sweater received by any of the boys up here so far and I show it with pride (and the bottom buttons of my field jacket closed). Most sweaters for soldiers are high-necked and must be worn under the shirt, but with a V-neck it can be worn outside the shirt under the field jacket. Did you get the floral offering I ordered for you for Easter?' he continued. 'I wanted it to be an orchid. It must have been wonderful to be in New York on Easter.'

He had a fairly eventful time himself. Although he was thousands of miles away from the war, ther were a number of invasion scares on the West Coast. On 8 April 1942 seven people died of heart attacks and an air-raid warden fell off the roof of a building when Los Angeles was blacked out for almost two hours due to the approach of some unidentified aeroplanes, which turned out to be friendly. On the Saturday before Easter, Johnny Dwyer and a couple of fellow officers were invited to a spaghetti dinner at the home of the local police chief at Sequim when an invasion scare began in the state of Washington. 'A messenger came running in to tell us that all officers were wanted at once,' he noted. 'We dashed off, leaving our host (the chief of police) and his wife and friends gaping. The story we heard outside the house was that there were hostile forces landing all over the peninsula. I didn't believe it, but got ready anyway – with tear gas, bayonet, rifle, hunting knife and all the ammunition I could carry, and five sandwiches. To make it even better, one of my guards reported by phone that he had trapped a saboteur at the power dam. To make it short – about 5 am we reached the conclusion – no Japs – no fight – no sleep, and we went to church. The people of Sequim knew there was something doing, 'cause hundreds of trucks were moving through the town. They feel hurt 'cause we didn't sound the air alarm and black out the town. Nolan was convinced the Japs would ambush us on the way back to the Command Post from the police chief's cottage.'

The invasion jitters were widespread. In fact, they were even more prevalent in the East. His stepmother had recently been hospitalised for an operation. 'My Dad tells me that my mother isn't improving as well as might be hoped for,' Johnny wrote. 'I'm very sorry to hear that. I think that half of her trouble comes from worrying about the war. She's very conscious of Long Island's nearness to the sea and Europe by air.' This time he signed off his letter to Margaret: 'Remember there's a second looey who loves you and you call him – Johnnie D.'

'I was very much pleased to know that your orchid gave you so much pleasure,' Johnny wrote to Margaret on 18 April. 'Your note gave me quite a lift too, 'cause I'm always glad to hear from you. I think of you more often than you realise (or suspect from the number of letters I write). By the time you receive this I may be in another town in Washington, but of course I can't say where or when, but you'll receive any new postcards I come across. Last night's news about the air raids on Japan was welcome, wasn't it! Uncle Sam is sending the war right into Mr Tojo's backyard. I liked the way the radio announcer said that the Japs deplored the vicious attacks on their cultural centres, hospitals and schools. The announcer said that the report was true about the cultural centres since munitions plants and shipyards are the best-known examples of Japan's great culture. There has been no official confirmation from the United States army. Apparently the tall lean gent with the striped pants and the stars on his hat is just stroking his beard and looking wise. It's too bad they didn't start bombing the Japs months ago. Maybe the glorious defence of Bataan wouldn't have been so disastrous. But there must have been a reason, and Monday-morning quarterbacks won't win the war.' This time he wound up: 'Sending you my love I remain yours, Johnny.'

As their own relationship was developing by mail, they

had the complications of other past relationships. 'I had to write a letter to my ex-sweetheart (of four or five years ago), telling her that I was more in love than ever with a girl from Brooklyn and that the Valentine that I sent ex was not to be misunderstood as she seemed to want to,' Johnny wrote. 'A guy this far away has to be so darn careful what he does and says. I'm not in the spot that some fellows I know are in.' Wherever they were stationed, some of the men got married, and then when they were transferred they got married again without bothering to divorce, or even notify the other wife – or even wives, in some cases. 'They just can't come back alive,' Johnny wrote. 'A wife in New Jersey, or New York, another in Louisiana, or North Carolina, and one in Washington. Those guys are bigamists.'

Margaret had been informally engaged to a man who had his own insurance agency. Don Hudson was drafted after Pearl Harbour but managed to get deferments until April 1942 in order to organise for someone to take over his business. He was obviously not cut out for army life, because within a week he was hospitalised, with a broken wrist that he suffered while on kitchen duty. 'I was opening a loaf of bread,' he explained. 'Of course, that is done differently in the army – you set the bread up on end on the counter and come down with your fist [to give] a good hard crack on the other end; this pressure breaks open the wax paper and then you just take the bread out and repeat. Well, a fellow bumped into me and I missed the loaf of bread and came down on the edge of the counter with my wrist.'

'You know, we haven't talked about us for quite a while,

and you are such a placid soul, I never know whether you have cooled off or not,' Don Hudson wrote to Margaret at the start of his second week in the army. 'I don't know what to say about getting married. All these boys here, quite a few of them are married and they are going overseas, some of them make out fine and others not so well. If you give me the go signal and encouragement, that is all I need, otherwise I for myself would be perfectly content to be a private. So it's up to you. Incidentally if everything is OK, what do you say if I start sending you some money to bank. You know, darling, I should have bought you a ring but I have never saved a nickel in my life. But I am sure you are the proper inspiration. And I can't wait any longer to start an estate, especially if we are going to have a half a dozen nuisances running around. With all my love, Don.'

After his move to the state of Washington, Johnny's mail took some time to catch up with him, but Margaret did telephone him. 'You are the swellest girl in the world calling me up way out here, and I can't help liking the swellest girl just as much as possible. Please write soon. Love, Johnny.' New York was a particularly exciting city at the time, as Manhattan dominated American culture. It was not only the publishing centre of the United States but also a centre for the arts: theatre, musicals, ballet, opera – indeed the whole entertainment industry – as well as fashion and political opinion. It set the tone for the nation, as most of the major syndicated political columnists and gossip columnists were based in New York. It also contained the country's financial center. Wall Street became synonymous with finance, Madison Avenue with advertising, and Broadway with entertainment.

After working through the night, Margaret and her friends would frequently go to shows that featured people like Red Buttons, Ginger Rodgers, Gregory Peck, Jackie Gleason and Frank Sinatra. Some of the big Broadway shows at the time included *Yankee Doodle Dandy*, *Sons and Soldiers* and *Wine, Women and Song*, which was the last burlesque show before the administration of Mayor Fiorello La Guardia banned such productions. Hollywood was producing new movies like an assembly line, but New York – 'the city that never sleeps' – was the hub of the arts in the United States. World premières of the most popular movies were held in New York, with all the associated glitz and glamour. It was the centre of critical acclaim. If they could make it there, they could make it anywhere, in the words of the song 'New York, New York'.

The hours were so hectic in the midst of an even more hectic lifestyle that AT&T provided sleeping dormitories for the operators, so that if they wished to stay in town to attend some of the shows or go shopping, they could grab a few hours' sleep, without having to go home, before returning to work. At the time, Margaret was the main wage earner in her house, largely supporting her mother and younger sister on earnings of around $3,000 a year. 'You are certainly a slave, working the hours you do. I heartily sympathise with you,' Johnny wrote. 'What you said about two days with three hours' sleep reminds me of those happy days when I used to go to NYC on Saturday morning – see a show before noon, another in the afternoon, meet Ed Root and Ed Wagner – see another, go to the RCA building and see a radio show with Tom

Canning and then sit in the York bar till 3 AM, then wander downtown and finally reach the Hudson Terminal for a Newark train at 5 AM. Ah! Wotta life!! Then we'd hear early Mass and go to bed till noon.'

On 6 May 1942, the night that Margaret and the other operators were taking messages from the men surrendering at Corregidor, Don Hudson was writing to her about how trying he was finding army life. 'I have never been jerked around so much in my whole life as I have been the past week,' Don wrote. 'I sure did run into a lot of bad luck since I have been in the army. Getting KP duty and injuring my wrist. Then being sent over to the hospital, and having to fight my way out of there.'

5

'GOSH! LOOK WHAT I WROTE!'

Johnny Dwyer proposed to Margaret in a letter on 23
May 1942, but again he was feeling his way and did not
come right out with what he meant. 'About your very
nice remark in your last letter – about my not having
trouble in anything I undertake,' he wrote. 'Do you think
that goes for winning the heart and hand of Margaret
Harrigan when Uncle Sam permits me to put myself to
work full time on that undertaking? I'm asking you. I've
always liked her a lot (to say the least) since the night I
met her – January 23, 1939 – in Brooklyn on a cold and
very windy night. I think she had one of those funny
little hats with purple flowers on it – violets, I guess.
Earlier in the evening I had called Kathleen to say hello
– and in spite of my beard I was invited over to meet you.
I could hardly believe that anyone (M.H.) so nice could
treat me so nice – and it's been like that ever since. She
sends me candy, cookies and jellies, salt-water taffy (thank
you so much), a sweater (a little short), and letters and
phone calls at 2 AM. M.H. is the nicest girl in the world
– and I don't have to go further to find out. I'm on duty
in the Message Centre tonight. All I do is sit here and

try to look officious, as the officer of the day should. I hate to be so deceitful. If anything comes over the telephone, I'm supposed to know what to do. But nothing ever happens, so I'm going to lay my head on the desk by the phone and dream of you. So long, pal – till I can see you again, I'll send my love, Johnny.'

'The more I'm away from you and the more I see of others the more I hope for a favourable outlook on that question to you included in my last letter (which question you evaded very gracefully, I must say – darn it),' he wrote the following week. 'To sum it all up, I miss you much, like you more and more and want you most of all. Did you hear about the British raid on Germany announced today? Twelve hundred bombers from sixty airports raided Cologne for ninety minutes. Boy, oh boy, I'll bet that burned Adolf. The British losses were less than 5 per cent. That's really wonderful. They dropped 6 million pounds of bombs. That ain't hay. Do you recall FDR's speech about the Tokyo bombing? He said the planes came from Shangri-La. The German news broadcasts repeated the report and said that the location of Shangri-La and the description of the airbase were not yet available. The Japs are bombing China in earnest now to see where Shangri-La is. I guess it's symbolic that the "Rising Sun" is really setting on the "Lost Horizon". The privacy of our bachelor establishment has been sadly intruded on of late. More darn officers' wives spend their evenings here. Seems like there's a party every night. Mostly our New Jersey 114th friends. The 71st and 174th are going to gang up some night and parade in shorts and horrify them out of the building if they don't leave at a decent hour.

When I finished the last sentence somebody yelled "Air raid!" and pulled the switch. Five minutes of darkness followed. And now to bed – goodnight Margaret. All my love, Johnny.'

The following week he wrote with the news that he had been promoted to First Lieutenant, and the week after that he proposed again, this time in a clear, straightforward way. 'Hello, brown eyes!' he began his letter on 15 June. 'I'm looking at your picture and pretending it's you. Since you're so far away, I don't suppose you can hear me, but you probably have known for a long time what I've been saying to the picture – which has the same sweet and considerate personality as you have – just keeps those big brown eyes glued on me – but never talks back to me. I look in those big brown eyes (as I only wish I really could) and say, "I'm in love with you – I want you to be my sweetheart for keeps – Will you be the girl I'm going to marry – Soon, please God." What's the answer, Margaret? Gosh! Look what I wrote! I meant every word of it too – if you don't believe me, I'll have it recorded and send you the record to hear it with your own ears. PS Reading between the lines is OK, but plain talk is very reassuring – don't you think. Your last letter made me very happy – you said you were proud of my being promoted – the night I got the news I came into my room and the first thing I noticed was your picture and my own mother's. Both pictures seemed alive and almost beaming. Right then and there I determined to be worthy of you and my mother – I had Father Durbin bless my bars and I'm praying that I'll never lose that blessing. The bars you sent me are perfect and you can

76

bet they are very valuable to me – they are rare and hard to get – and you gave them to me. It was swell of you to go to so much trouble getting them for me. I'd like to send you a ring, but you'll have to tell me whether you'll take it or not and what size it should be.'

'I put off answering your letter for a few days so that I might give it some very serious thought,' Margaret replied on 20 June. 'By now I know myself well enough to realise that I hate to make important decisions, in fact I must always force myself to do so. After a proper amount of thought I should be very happy indeed to marry you. You will never know how hard I had to struggle with myself to write this. I thought I would call you 'cause I really do find it very difficult to write. Silly, isn't it. It would be wonderful if you were just a little bit nearer, for there are so many things to talk about. I will call you Thursday night if at all possible.'

'While I'm waiting for your call, I'm writing a letter,' Johnny wrote on 25 June. 'And a letter to you. I particularly enjoy writing because I'm thinking of someone very special when I'm thinking of you. Your last letter told me the news I've wanted to hear. Asking you across the whole width of the country wasn't so good as asking you in person would be, but then maybe I would find myself stuttering and end up by asking you something else, or maybe you wouldn't answer me right away and then where would we be?'

'I'm really living for that day when I can go about my soldiering with the feeling that I'm fighting for someone special – my own "better half" and a "home" of our own,' Johnny wrote on 5 July. He wrote to Kathleen and Jules

Coelos with the news to express how much he appreciated them introducing Margaret to him. 'I really meant it,' he wrote. 'Kathleen can or probably has told you a lot about me that I don't talk about any more.' He added that she '"came through" as a friend to me at a time when I really needed a lot of moral uplifting. She was swell.' Kathleen had obviously told Margaret some of the story, but she would not learn for some time that he was obviously scarred by what he felt had been the rejection of his stepmother. He referred to her in a normal way in his letters, referring to her as his 'Mother', and did not use the term 'stepmother', but he distinguished her from his real mother by referring to the latter as 'my own Mother'. 'My Dad has offered me my (own) Mother's ring, which he says we can have made to your liking – whatever setting you like. Wouldn't it be swell if we were only together to talk these things over. He had the ring and another like it for himself made out of five British gold pieces. I would like you to have my Mother's ring if you would like it. If you talk to my Dad on the phone, he could probably tell you what it's all about. We can talk about it when you call. All my love, Johnny.

Margaret met Johnny's father and stepmother shortly afterwards. 'She is a very clever girl and apparently has a responsible position with correspondingly high salary, and she told us she had been in Europe and has been on the road travelling for her company,' Jack Dwyer wrote to Johnny afterwards. 'He said that he understands that you are the sole support of your mother and sister and to his way of thinking it would be unfair to all concerned for you to give up your good position to marry me and take up temporary quarters here, there and everywhere until I get permanently located,' Johnny wrote to Margaret on 12 August. 'Now I know my Dad and I know his reasoning. He wants me to marry you, but he wants us to be happy and to have the best living conditions to found our home life on – in which we all agree. Of course I never asked you how the economic structure of the Harrigan family is built, but regardless of how, I want to marry Margaret Harrigan and share her "problems", if any, and to get myself another swell sister and mother. As to the living here, there and everywhere, you have your own ideas about that, I know. Also I've noticed the tribe of army wives are a surprisingly carefree crowd – though a separate segment in the society of the community if they don't make themselves a part of it all. As to the temporary nature of my duty here. Well, I may alone or with the regiment be sent to Alaska or Australia any time on a day's notice or less. Now the question: When I'm able to arrange it, will you come out here to me – even if it's only for a little while – either for your own reason or for Uncle Sam's? I do want you to stay with me – though we may have to get a tent, with housing the way it is in Seattle – though we won't be right here indefinitely. Elsewhere around here it's not so bad. If we can do it (the surprise I've been working on), we could take that five days' leave of mine for a honeymoon trip somewhere out here in the beautiful West. Even to Canada.'

Johnny and Margaret talked on the telephone on 17 August, but he was distinctly inhibited, because the telephone that he was using was between the rooms of two Majors. 'One is a pain in the neck,' he explained. 'If

79

those darned Majors weren't in tonight, I could have told you so much more. The pain would have taken a delight in changing any plans I might discuss with you, though, so I'm very unhappy about that. You see why I couldn't talk on the army phone,' he continued. 'Usually when you call, they leave a message to call back and I get into a booth phone.' He and one of the Second Lieutenants had been having problems with the Major, who was the commanding officer of the outfit. 'The latest thing was the fact that I'm too noisy at night,' Johnny explained. 'Yesterday about 3 AM when I was staggering in from a guard inspection, I dropped my helmet and it sounded like a ton of bricks bouncing around.' He wrote a couple of pages explaining what he would have liked to have said, but then he 'decided they weren't so good, for one reason or another. Altogether they added up to, "Don't let my stepmother ever scare you" and "I love you very much."'

The surprise he was planning was a hundred-and-fifty-dollar bank loan for six months to enable them to get married in September. He sent Margaret the money to come out to Seattle, where they would be married. 'You've done quite a bit of travelling about this big land, so you probably know what's what about that,' he wrote. 'Now if we were Polish, we could have everything arranged for us, like my company mechanic. He and his girlfriend were surprised to find that the Polish Home Society had a party and three hundred guests, orchestra, food, cake and everything prepared – even hired a hall. The photographer was there for the usual Polish wedding picture and also to put a five-column photo in the Seattle newspaper.

Write to me real soon and tell me what I should do out here,' he continued.

He had already informed his father of their plans. Margaret was going to come out to Seattle, where they would be married, and she would stay for about a month. She would then return to New York, where she would go back to work with AT&T. 'Any time you talk to him, you don't have to hold anything back unless I previously told you to – because my Dad has always let me think and plan my own doings, whether they concur with his opinions or not,' Johnny wrote. 'Gosh, Margaret, I'm more excited than I was when I graduated from school or at any other time in my life.'

For Margaret, however, it was a particularly trying period. As well as handling calls about the Allied disaster at Dieppe, she had to inform both Syd Ritterman and Don Hudson of her plans to get married. Both of them were anxious to marry her. 'I am fed up and wish I was back home, even though I would have to work hard, and maybe get you to say "yes",' Syd wrote to her on 27 June 1942. 'If there was any doubt in my mind previously, there isn't any now, so say "no" to the other two.'

'Boy, have I got it bad!' he wrote on 15 August. 'If you haven't anything to do, ask Mom if I can get into the family. Let me know what she says.' Syd was not surprised, however, when she telephoned him about her plans to get married. 'I was hit by the news of your coming marriage, even though I had some sort of inkling that there was something coming off by the infrequent answers of your letter,' he wrote to her a couple of days later. 'Once again, let me wish you all the happiness in the

81

world because if there is anybody who deserves it, you do, and if anything goes wrong I want you to let me know, because there will always be a spark of you with me. Always yours, Syd. PS If you want to travel to Virginia instead of Seattle, it's OK with me.'

Margaret tried but failed to get Don Hudson on the telephone. He also sensed that something was wrong. 'If I have written anything in my letters that has gotten your dander up or changed your feeling towards me, or if there is any reason for your sudden lack of interest, won't you please write me a note and let me know, as I am much concerned,' he wrote on 20 August. 'Be frank, dear, is there anything wrong?'

He wrote again eleven days later: 'I naturally was quite surprised when I received your letter yesterday. I tried to get you by phone but after waiting for a line to NY for three and a half hours, I gave up in disgust. And you have to wait around the pay station in the Post Exchange – and there are always fifty to seventy-five men waiting to call somewhere. The telephone situation is entirely inadequate for the size of the camp. Well, to get back to the subject (which is a difficult thing to do), naturally I was speechless all day yesterday and today. But it seems that I can think clearly now – that is, as clear as anyone could under the circumstances. Naturally your well-being and happiness is my foremost desire. If he loves you (which I really believe he does) and you love him, then there will be only one person unhappy.

'I will pray fervently that you may be guided by the Blessed Mother what to do. You mean so much to me, that regardless what you would ever do, I would never be angry with you. Hurt perhaps, dejected naturally, but never angry. My only desire is your complete happiness. As long as I know you are happy, I will be somewhat content. You mean more to me than anything in the whole wide world. I have never felt so near to anyone in this whole world. Please for our sake don't make a wrong decision. . . . Please explore the situation fully and if there is the slightest question in your mind as to your wholehearted love for him, for God's sake postpone it or call it off. Because you will only make all three of us miserable eventually. Don't consider this a sales talk on my part, as I don't intend it to be. Don't make your decision between us but whether you should or should not marry him. Do you love him? Or aren't you sure? That is your decision to make. Many people are hastily getting married, don't let yourself be caught in a whirl-pool. Because soon you can make another decision about me. I don't believe that any couple that have had as much enjoyment as we have had together are not suited for each other. Love, Don.'

'I wish I'd asked you about three years sooner,' Johnny wrote on 8 September. 'You see, I wanted to ask you way back then, but I was afraid I might spoil the friendship, or make you think I was a "wolf". I still remember the night I met you and how worried I was that the shave I needed might completely spoil your opinion of me.'

The following Saturday Margaret set out for Seattle by train. She left shortly before midnight. Johnny's father and stepmother were at Grand Central Station to see her off, along with Margaret's mother, Therese, and a couple of close family friends. The first part of the journey to

Chicago was uneventful. Margaret went to the club car but it was packed, so she went to bed early. The next day she teamed up with Rosalia Lynch from Paterson, New Jersey, and they went to the club car. 'We were able to get a seat, thank goodness,' she wrote. 'The people aboard are very uninteresting and to make it worse they are selling the seats in the club car. So we went to lunch and then stayed in our own car.' After a sixteen-hour trip, they arrived in Chicago. During the stopover in the Windy City, she took a cab into the Loop to go to the movies. 'The only picture I had not seen was *I Married an Angel*,' she wrote. It was the latest – and, turned out, the last – of the series of movies starring Nelson Eddy and Janette MacDonald. 'It was enjoyable,' Margaret said.

Around 11 PM she telephoned the office in New York and talked to some of her colleagues. 'It was good to talk to someone from home,' she noted. 'I don't mind admitting I am lonesome. Hope the rest of the trip is better than the first part.' On the second leg of the journey she made friends with a group of people who taught her to play gin rummy. They ate their meals together and drank some beer to break up the trip. One little girl's grandmother became ill, so Margaret took care of the girl for the older woman. Two of the people Margaret made friends with were Lieutenant Frank Wallace and Mildred Gouch. On the Tuesday morning they all had breakfast together as they were passing through the Rocky Mountains. 'We went out on the observer platform and the view was wonderful,' she wrote. 'Frank is trying to talk me out of marrying Johnny and marrying him. It's fun.' They passed through Glacier National Park, where the scenery was 'indescribable', according to Margaret.

6

STARTING A FAMILY

Margaret Harrigan and John Gerald Dwyer were married
in the Cathedral of St James in Seattle, Washington, at
nine o'clock on the morning of 21 September 1942. It
was a tiny wedding, consisting of just five people in total:
the bride and groom, the two witnesses and the Catholic
chaplain, who performed the ceremony in the large
church. The best man was Captain Paul Maloney, a
medical doctor with the unit, and the matron of honour
was Major John Keider, the 'nosy major' about whom
Johnny had complained in his letters. Afterwards they
spent the wedding night in the Olympic Hotel, where
Bob Hope, Frances Langford and Jerry Colona were
staying before setting off for Alaska as part of the United
Services Organisation's tour of military bases. Margaret
and Johnny actually met them in an elevator that night.

The next day the newlyweds headed for the Olympic
Peninsula, where they spent their honeymoon in the
village of Sequim, staying in the local inn. At the end of
the two-week holiday, Margaret flew back to Chicago,
from where she took a train to New York; she went back
to work on 12 October. The most memorable aspect of

her return journey was her first flight. It was a DC4 aircraft and she was sitting next to a congressman from Washington who was making his way back to the capital. 'I was having a terrible time keeping awake and the congressman was busy telling me that everybody got sick the first time they flew,' Margaret wrote. 'He kept waking me up to tell me I should be getting sick.' They hit a thunderstorm over the Rockies, but it was very calm the rest of the way. 'He woke me up ten minutes out of Chicago to say that his friend "always got sick" ten minutes out of Chicago,' she recalled. 'Such a dope! I think he was terrified of flying and he was trying to terrify me. The altitude had affected me to the extent that I couldn't keep awake.' She never did get airsick that day – or any other time she travelled by air.

'I can't remember when time passed so slowly,' Johnny wrote from Boeing Field, Washington, on 26 October. 'It seems like a year since you left me. And it's really still part of the same month.'

'This afternoon I saw Wake Island,' he continued. 'I was thinking as I saw the one fellow take leave of his wife, and another take leave of his daughter, how lucky we are to be separated by our own country and not by the Pacific Ocean and the Jap fleet. Let's hope that the same ocean doesn't get in between us for a long, long time yet.' Being attached to the Western Defence Command rather than the Army Ground Forces 'would indicate that we are at least temporarily a fixture in this locale,' he wrote. He added that there were rumours that his unit might be transferred to Port Angeles, but he warned her not to mention this to any of the intelligence men with whom she was working. The following day he mentioned having heard a speech by Wendell Willkie, whom Roosevelt had beaten in the 1940 presidential election. Johnny was greatly impressed with Willkie. 'He certainly carried some dynamite,' he wrote. 'It appears to me that he's heading for some kind of big time – he will doubtless run for president again. He has the gruff, sincere sort of friendly attitude that makes him popular with un-sophisticated people. He is really more like a man of the people than FDR. I saw him in Newark once, and he is a most likeable sort of person. If only he had been more on the ball, he'd go places for sure.'

Politically, Margaret and Johnny were probably poles apart, as she was a fervent admirer of Roosevelt, but they were separated by the width of the United States on election day 1942 and by the width of the Atlantic Ocean two years later when Roosevelt was elected to a fourth term as president. 'Goodnight, my darling,' Johnny concluded in his letter of 27 October. 'I'm afraid this is one of those nights when I'll keep my promise not to wake you up again.'

In New York Margaret worked at AT&T for a further six months, until Johnny was transferred to the Infantry School at Fort Benning, Georgia, in February 1943. Margaret then resigned her job at AT&T. Johnny was due to go to Georgia via his old home in Bethlehem, Pennsylvania, where Margaret went to meet him. Train travel was chaotic at the time. Priority was given to trains carrying military supplies, with the result that passenger trains were often shunted into sidings for hours at a time. People travelling all the way from the West Coast were therefore subject to long delays: Johnny was three days late arriving in Bethlehem. During her stay with the family in Bethlehem, Margaret met Johnny's grandmother and three maiden aunts – Mary, Nellie and Elizabeth – but she only once briefly saw his eldest uncle, Patrick, who went to work early every morning in the steel mills. His mother doted on him but he did not eat with the rest of the family, with the result that Margaret never coincided with him.

Johnny's grandmother, who was in her nineties, was one of the worst cooks that Margaret ever encountered. She ran the kitchen and would not allow any of her daughters to prepare food. Margaret began to suffer terrible indigestion and, in later life, she often wondered if she had got an ulcer while waiting there. She concluded that his grandmother's cooking probably explained why Johnny never seemed to have any real interest in food. After the brief stay in Pennsylvania, she and Johnny went to live in Columbus, Georgia, which was near Fort Benning. Margaret got a job as a telephone operator with Southern Bell. When Johnny completed his infantry course, on 18 May 1943, he was assigned to the 174th Infantry, headquartered in San Fernando, California, and the couple moved back west. They made the trip by train: it was another arduous journey. Their train was repeatedly put into sidings in Alabama, with the result that it took over two days to get New Orleans. They had planned to spend a night there, but they were so late that they had already missed the train that they had intended to connect with, and they ended up spending three days in New Orleans before they could get a reservation on a train to

California. They booked a drawing room, but they ended up in an upper bunk. 'That we weren't divorced by the time we got to California was a miracle, 'cause two people in an upper bunk ain't great,' Margaret noted. 'It was miserable. There wasn't room to move.'

On returning to his regiment, Johnny found that the men had magnificent suntans. They had been used as extras in the Irving Berlin movie *This Is the Army*. Wearing make-up was considered out of the question, so instead the men tanned themselves in the sun, which was not difficult in southern California. The future senator George Murphy was the star of *This Is the Army*, in which future president Ronald Reagan played Murphy's son. The show had been a great hit on Broadway. Many members of the army, including Ronald Reagan, then an army lieutenant, were part of the cast. Berlin had recruited soldiers for the Broadway show in Camp Upton, New York. The whole thing was actually a reworking of his First World War show *Yip, Yip Yaphank*. That show had begun with minstrels (white actors with their faces painted black), but in the new show Berlin decided to use black soldiers instead. At the time, the army was still segregated; the cast for *This Is the Army* became the army's first integrated company. The Broadway show was the biggest and best-known American morale-boosting show of the Second World War, with songs like 'This is the Army, Mr Brown' and 'Oh, How I Hate to Get Up in the Morning', which was sung by Berlin himself. The piece was a show within a show, in which supposed army entertainers were moving about entertaining the forces.

The First Lady, Eleanor Roosevelt, saw the show three

times and was largely responsible for persuading the company to take it to Washington, DC, so that the president could see it. But this posed some security problems. There was one scene in which a soldier on kitchen patrol was wielding a meat cleaver, but the president's security people did not want anyone within fifteen feet of the president with a cleaver, so the scene was changed. It was also decided that the cast would present arms rather than take theatrical bows at the end. As Irving Berlin came on stage from the left at the end of the show, the director, Ezra Stone, was to give the order 'Eyes left!' to the cast. But as Berlin was coming on stage, he realised that the president was to the right, so he ordered 'Right face!' At that point the cast turned their backs on the sensitive Berlin, who was mortally offended. He accused Stone of deliberately humiliating him in front of the president of the United States. Berlin later upbraided the director, who was Jewish, in front of the other members of the company. Even though Berlin was the son of a Jewish cantor himself, he complained that there were 'too many Jews in the show'. He said that the cast gave the appearance that Jews were trying to avoid combat duty by appearing in a morale-boosting show.

Many new soldiers were drafted in for the shooting of the movie, which was spiced up with the addition of Kate Smith to sing 'God Bless America'. The world heavyweight boxing champion, Joe Louis, also had a cameo part. Soldiers from the 174th Infantry Regiment occupied a ten-acre campsite near the studio. They lived in electrified tents constructed by the studio's prop department. Each day they would march in formation to the studio and report for duty where they were assigned. Then at the end of the day they marched back to their camp. While on duty at the studio, they were not permitted to approach any of the actresses, but off-duty was a different matter. It was possibly as a result of the role of the 174th in *This Is the Army* that the regiment's badge was later used by the unit in the long-running television series *Sergeant Bilko*. Or maybe it was just one of the props left over from the movie.

Johnny was not involved with the movie. He and Margaret got an apartment together in Inglewood, California, which Margaret described as 'pretty God-awful'. Johnny was often gone for two or three days at a time, and she knew no one in the area, so she found it very lonely. The various officers' wives were scattered around Los Angeles, which even then was a sprawling city. When Johnny's unit was moved further north, they got an apartment in Ventura, California, but it was not much better.

By this time, Margaret's mother had got a permanent nursing position, and once school was out in June 1943, Therese came out to live with Margaret and Johnny. Shortly afterwards, Johnny's unit was transferred to Ojai, California, which was a tiny town of a little over two thousand people on the other side of the first mountain range in from the ocean. 'It was absolutely gorgeous,' Margaret recalled. 'It was only eight miles in from the coast but it was over the first lines of the Rockies. The town was so small that all of the officers lived near each other in a number of holiday homes, and they formed lasting family friendships.'

'There was a great social life there, because the headquarters was the Ojai Country Club,' Margaret remembered. 'They had a beautiful bar, dining room and everything. We got invited to dinner at the officers' mess very often – all the wives and children – and we met all the people in the company.' It was in Ojai that Margaret met Mike Hession, who told her the story about delivering booze while wheeling the pram containing the daughter of a Mrs Harrigan.

There was a superb golf course at the Ojai Country Club, but there was nobody playing, because the army had taken over the course. They had tents and equipment on what had been the fairways. Margaret and the others did most of their shopping in Ventura, but midway between it and Ojai there was a roadside store that sold apple juice in one-gallon glass containers. Johnny, being a chemist, came up with the idea of mixing raisins with the apple juice. He would then allow the concoction to sit in the sun in the hundred-and-thirty-degree heat for three days, and it would turn into hard cider. 'We didn't have to buy any booze, 'cause we made our own,' Margaret laughed. 'Every party you had, that was the drink, and it was very pleasant. You put it in the fridge to make it cold. It was very alcoholic.'

When the 174th moved south to the Los Angeles area, they had to find a new place. Answering a classified advertisement about something completely different, Margaret met an extremely wealthy woman who happened to own a large beach house at Manhattan Beach, and she persuaded her to rent it to a group of them. It was a kind of patriotic gesture on the woman's part, helping young soldiers. Three families, consisting of eight people, moved into the three-storey house, which was built on the side of a steep slope overlooking the beach. From the roadside, it was just a two-storey house with a three-car garage, but at the front it went down another level. It was an idyllic setting. In addition to Margaret, Johnny and Therese, Jim and Molly Moore lived there, as well as Jim and Jean Root and their baby, Larry.

It was a fourteen-room house, magnificently furnished with California mission furniture. There was a huge living room and a dining room, off which was a balcony. There was also a magnificent kitchen, with exquisite selections of services in mission ware for about fifty or sixty people. 'There were whole sets of pink and whole sets of blue, and pale orange,' Margaret noted. 'It was gorgeous. You would look at the sunset and decide what colour you would set the table with.' They appreciated the woman's generosity. 'We left the place absolutely perfect,' Margaret added. 'We didn't do any damage at all. We didn't break anything, even. We were very, very careful, because we did appreciate her renting it. She had no notion of renting, but we were desperate.'

The three men were transferred to Camp White, near Medford, Oregon, in February 1944. 'The town of Medford is absolutely unimpressive,' Johnny wrote on 12 February 1944. 'The men state that it would be cruelty to make them stay twenty-four hours in the town. I was there last night for about twenty minutes. I felt depressed by the place and came back to the bright and cheerful army camp by 8.45 PM.'

The 174th Infantry regiment was no longer part of the Western Defense Command. 'We are now Army

Ground Forces troops,' Johnny explained. They were told that they were going to be transferred to Alaska or Hawaii on the way to the Pacific front. 'Our boys seem to be doing great things in the Pacific,' Johnny wrote. 'The casualties aren't as bad as were expected. It seems that the worst trouble is from malaria, which the army is trying to educate us on.' Although they were told that none of the wives could go to Oregon, because the men were to be transferred to the Pacific shortly, they soon learned that this was only a ruse by Lt Col Collins to send his wife back to New York. He had concocted the story to suit himself. When the wives were entertained by the wife of the commanding officer of the regiment, Major General Parker, they learned that the move was not an indication of imminent transfer to the Pacific and there was no reason why they could not join their husbands. Had they known in time, they could have travelled in the military convoy, but now they had to make their own way in the one car that they all shared.

Margaret did most of the driving over some treacherous roads. The three wives, Therese and the baby, Larry, broke the trip in San Francisco, arriving at the swanky Mark Hopkins Hotel in a beat-up 1936 Chevrolet, overloaded with luggage. Instead of being sent to the Far East, Johnny was moved to Camp Chaffee in Fort Smith, Arkansas, in March 1944. At the time, Margaret was almost eight months pregnant. 'You have no idea how I hate the Japs, Germans and New York politicians for making me move away from Margaret at this time,' Johnny wrote to Margaret's mother on 16 April 1944. Although the baby was not due for over a week, Margaret began to experience

cramps on Wednesday 19 April. 'By 4 PM they were coming every ten minutes, and by 5 PM every five minutes,' she wrote afterwards. 'The doctor told me when I was having hard pains every ten minutes or so to get to the hospital.' But she thought it was a false alarm because the cramps did not actually turn into pains, so she and Therese carried on as normal. 'We went out to dinner and then to a movie,' Margaret wrote. 'How the people in back of me saw the picture I don't know, as I was jumping around a bit.' John Keider, who had been one of the witnesses at their wedding, thought this was very funny. 'Thumper kicked the back out of the seat and then quieted down for the final big push,' he joked.

'We came home and went to bed, but I was getting these cramps every five minutes but no pains,' Margaret continued. 'Well, I got up and sat on the chair. Tess was sound asleep. I had the radio on low, then got out a book Alice Cross lent me on prenatal care. It said that the pains were cramp-like. So I got my clothes ready and washed and got dressed, woke up Tess and told her I was going to the hospital. Called the Red Cross and they said they would be over in twenty minutes. I gave Tess money and a cheque and warnings on eating. She wanted to come with me but I would be worried about her out there and I told her the baby would not be born until morning and she could call and find out.

'First time in my life I had a police escort. A police car came with the Red Cross car. They took us, with both car sirens blaring and red lights flashing, to the edge of town. Then the Red Cross car went sixty miles an hour out to the camp. It was really very exciting. When I got there a boy put me in a wheelchair and raced me miles through the hospital halls. The doctor examined me and said that nothing was doing for a while, so I was getting kinda disgusted, 'cause I wanted it over with . . . Nothing was as I expected. I kept waiting for pains in my stomach. All of a sudden the nurse came in with a mask on and wheeled me into the delivery room. They gave me ether after they had me sign for a spinal. When I woke up it was all over.'

That night in Arkansas Johnny was awakened by a telephone call at about 11.30. 'To say the least I was worried, because no one ever has occasion to phone me here,' he wrote. 'Then I recognised the voice of Corporal Reed at Message Centre. He said he had a telegram for me, and then he read it: "Boy arrived 12.45 PM both fine weight six lbs eight and a half ounces, Therese." The corporal then congratulated him. 'I had to hear it again to make sure it was what I really heard,' Johnny continued. 'I couldn't go to sleep then and had to take a walk to get calm again. I stopped in our regiment club for a Coke and a game of ping-pong, after which I announced the good news to those present.'

Margaret did not actually get to see the baby until the following day. 'They don't bring the babies out of the nursery for twelve hours,' she explained in a letter to her mother the next day. 'I haven't seen Thumper yet. I can't call him Ryle until I see him. Eight days ahead of time isn't too bad. He is such a homely little thing . . . [He] looked like a little peanut. The only thing you can recognise about him is a dimple in his chin.'

'It's wonderful that everything turned out so well – I mean a boy, just as you predicted and we both wanted,' Johnny wrote. 'Everybody wants to know if it's "Junior", and I say, no "Junior". Whatever you say goes – just so it isn't Elmer or Reginald or such. I know darn well it won't be.'

'It was swell to nominate Owenie as godfather for "Thumper",' he added. He asked if Therese was going to be godmother. 'Tess ought to be in on the launching, I think, don't you? We had a cocktail party Friday afternoon. Only the 3rd Battalion and Canon Company officers were in this one. We didn't have so much to drink. Being the new father, they told the bartender to take care of me. He did all right on the first one. But the second one I got was made for John D. It was about nine-tenths rum. That was all I had. It was a good thing too. Then the whole bunch went to the movies to see Lucille Ball in some defence-worker stage-girl picture. It was good, I think. I had a wonderful time, 'cause Keider was higher than a kite and three times as funny. I hit the hay early and slept quite well. Once a week is enough of that.'

Therese had also sent a telegram to her mother, who promptly telephoned for further details and could not understand why Therese had not yet visited the hospital. Mary told her to go to the hospital at once. She did not realise that the army hospital was ten miles from town. Therese, then still only sixteen years old, had never driven a motor car, but she took the car all the same. When she pulled into a filling station, the attendant – a one-armed veteran – realised that she should not be driving. She did not even know how to find reverse. He got into the car, showed her the different gears and gave her a driving lesson around the filling-station forecourt. She then drove out to the hospital by herself.

Johnny Dwyer had thought that his unit was going to be moved to Hawaii but that proved to be a false rumour. He hoped to make arrangements for Margaret, Therese and the baby to stay in the Fort Smith area, but he was unable to get a suitable place. 'About a house or apartment, I don't know what to tell you,' he wrote to Margaret. 'Best to use your own judgement when you see them. Down here the situation is funny.'

When the 174th Infantry was moving to Arkansas, the men and their families travelled by road in a military convoy. As the military had priority at the time, the trip was relatively easy from the point of view of obtaining petrol, oil or tyres. If any of the cars broke down, there were plenty of mechanics to help with repairs, or men to change any tyres. Moreover, there was no problem in obtaining a tyre in the event of a blow-out.

Margaret's doctor had ordered her not to make the arduous journey to Arkansas until after the baby was born and she had recovered from the birth. Therese was enrolled in high school in Medford, so it was easier for her to stay where she was, with Margaret. The school year was already nearing its end on Friday 26 May when Margaret and Therese left Medford with the five-week-old baby, heading for Arkansas. They were travelling in a blue 1936 Chevrolet sedan. The army had provided ration coupons for petrol, oil and tyres. Neither Margaret nor Therese had ever got a driver's licence, but they did have insurance to drive.

The car was in good shape, but the tyres were bad. At the time, civilians could not buy new tyres; only retreads were available, and some of those should never have been recycled, as they were in very poor condition. After crossing into California, they were stopped by the police near Redding, but the cop left them off with a caution when Margaret promised to get a licence.

They spent the first of four California stops in Redding, with the others in Stockton, Bakersfield and Barstow in the Mojave Desert, which was a particularly memorable experience. Each morning Margaret would pack the baby's bottles in ice. Passing through the desert, it was about a hundred and thirty degrees. 'We stopped in Mojave to have a woman in a roadside store heat the bottle,' Margaret said. 'She thought I was out of my mind – a hundred and thirty degrees!'

That night they stayed in a motel in Barstow, which 'was terrible,' Margaret noted. All the legs of the furniture were placed in cans of creosol and there were warnings placed around the room advising patrons not to attempt to put on their shoes without first shaking them out, because of the danger of scorpions. Once they turned out the light, they could hear the scorpions dragging their tails across the wooden floor, so they turned the light back on and kept it on for the rest of the night.

Crossing through the Mojave Desert and Death Valley, they had to move in short stages, but once they got into Arizona and New Mexico they were able to travel further each day. At the time, many servicemen were hitchhiking, and they usually picked them up, as it was very difficult for them to get a lift.

They spent a night in Kingmon, Arizona, then moved on to Albuquerque, New Mexico, where they had the hair-raising experience of getting caught in a dust storm while travelling through what was essentially desert. They had picked up a young soldier who was on his way back to Texas. He was sitting on the front seat beside Margaret, while Therese was in the back with the baby. As they were going down a steep incline, they experienced a blow-out. Margaret went for the brake and the car began to veer off the road. If they had gone off the road at that point, the car would probably have rolled, and they might well have been killed. 'Keep your foot off the brake and ride it out!' the soldier shouted as he held on to the steering wheel. Eventually they came to rest naturally. The soldier then put on the spare tyre. A posse came along on horses, like the real Wild West, and they told them the nearest town where they could get another spare tire. The following day they had another blow-out. In all they had three blow-outs on the trip. On the other two occasions, truck drivers stopped and changed the tyre for them. Neither Margaret nor Therese knew how to change a tyre, but 'the truckers were absolutely marvellous,' Margaret recalled. Each time, however, they would have go to a ration board at the next town to get permission to buy another Grade 3, retread tire. The board would have to get together: one might be the local undertaker, another the barber, and so on.

When the two women reached Oklahoma City, Johnny met them. He had taken a bus from Fort Smith. He then drove the last leg of the journey – though not without some further drama when they ran out of gasoline in the middle of nowhere. They stayed in Fort Smith, living in the Doldman Hotel. Arkansas was very backward in comparison with a developing state like California. People living in the Ozarks were living in dreadful squalor and poverty. They also had a high incidence of venereal disease. As a result, the army tried to keep as many men as possible on base for the weekend by providing entertainment in the form of movies or other activities, including aircraft and glider flights and parachute jumps.

The housing available in Fort Smith was substandard, so Margaret decided to return to New York with Therese and the baby after about a month in Arkansas. They travelled by train. Johnny followed on for a two-week furlough. 'My two weeks in Brooklyn with you and Ryle were two of the happiest in my whole life,' Johnny wrote to Margaret on 23 July, following his return to Arkansas. 'I have such a wonderful wife and we have the most wonderful baby in the world. Even if he is supposed to look like his Dad, he's not a homely baby like somebody said. I wish you were both here.'

In the same letter, he mentioned that he had just received an indication that he was about to be sent overseas. 'At lunchtime today, one of the boys slapped me on the back and said, "I see you made it." I am to take a physical examination tomorrow along with about thirty more.' While many of the men in his unit were sent to the Pacific, Johnny Dwyer was sent to the 'European Theatre of Operations'. This made more sense in his case, as he had four years of high school French and had studied German at university. He was not supposed to say where he was going, but when he was transferred and ordered to report to the New York area, it was obvious that it was not going to be the Pacific. This afforded him another opportunity to spend time at home.

'It was wonderful being with you the other night,' he wrote to Margaret on 15 August 1944. 'It was too bad it had to be so short a time. You have no idea how much it means to me to know I have you and Ryle waiting.' This was his last letter from the United States. He was in New York City but, for security reasons, could not make contact with his wife. The troops were carried to Britain on converted ocean liners like the *Queen Mary, Queen Elizabeth, Mauritania* and *Île de France*. These would carry about ten thousand troops on each sailing, so there were extreme security measures to prevent any hint of news of the sailing getting to the enemy.

'Like everybody else I have been trying to think of a clever way to tell you just about where I am,' Johnny wrote. 'But you shouldn't know anyway, so I won't tell you. You'd be annoyed and disappointed, too, if I told you. By the time you read this, I'll be writing from a much greater distance. I'll try to write to you every day, but you know I may be occupied with a lot of little things I don't know about now. But sweetie, please, even if I don't write regularly, please drop me a line often. And send me pictures of yourself and the baby.' He wrote several letters on the boat, the *Île de France*, though he never actually mentioned where he was. The most he wrote of his whereabouts was simply 'Some Place'.

On the boat, he saw Bing Crosby's show and met and talked with him. Crosby, who was on his way to Europe to entertain the troops, was probably the hottest entertainer in show business at the time. His film *Going My Way* was the biggest box-office success of the year. It went on to win the Oscar for best movie, and Crosby won the award for best actor. In addition, he had a whole series of number-one songs that year. 'I Love You' topped the charts during May and June 1944, while 'I'll Be Seeing You,' was number one in July, and 'Swinging on a Star,' hit the top as Crosby was crossing the Atlantic and would remain there for the next two months. He performed four shows a day for the troops on board the ship in the course of the eight-day voyage.

The men also provided their own entertainment. 'During the trip we had a lot of fun with one fellow who had learned a lot about hypnotism while he was in school,' Johnny wrote following his arrival in England. 'Every night we'd get the room full and he'd invite any sceptics to sit on the floor in front of him. He'd indicate a spot on the wall to be watched and then he'd proceed to induce sleep. He put six to sleep at once one night. Then he'd have them do all sorts of tricks while in that state. He induced illusions and fantasies, which were remarkable. One night he had a fighter pilot take him up for a ride. They stunted, he got "sick", had conversations with the pilot – even landed the plane on one wheel. There were other pilots around who said the man's behavior was perfect. He flicked all the switches and watched his meters and so on, just like the real thing. He even called the tower on the radio to get clearance for the flying field. Another fellow toured Washington, DC, in a Model T Ford car. He went to buy gas – got in trouble because his tickets were counterfeit – and he paid ten dollars for six gallons of gas. When he came to, he was surprised to find his ten dollars missing from his wallet.'

The troops arrived in Greenock, Scotland, and were

taken by train to southern England, where military conditions were relaxed. 'After lunch we were scheduled for a hike of some two hours' duration,' he wrote on 29 August. 'It took fifteen minutes or less to get out of sight, and the game of African dominoes taught everyone a great deal about making change with English money.'

'I'll bet two of these dirty brown ones [pennies],' one soldier would say. 'Two square ones,' somebody else would bet. That was the old many-sided threepenny-bit. They called a shilling 'a little one' and a half-crown 'a big one'. After their two-hour 'hike,' they returned to camp. For weeks, Johnny waited in vain for his mail to catch up with him. As a First Lieutenant, he was censoring his men's mail, so he realised that the other men had the same problems. 'I haven't left camp, as there isn't much to see or buy,' he wrote from 'somewhere in England' on 1 September 1944. For military reasons he was never able to say specifically where he was at any time. 'The boys brought back some amazing stories about Bath,' he reported. They watched one girl at the railway station pick up four soldiers, neck a while and fervently kiss them goodbye. Another was a trifle hurt when they told her she'd probably sent more men off to camp than Ike had sent over to France.

'I spent all day today censoring mail, and believe me it's no picnic,' he wrote three days later. 'It's very depressing to read some of the b—s— and trash some of them write to family and girlfriends. Some of them are downright lies and malicious rumors. But we are not censors of morals or literacy . . . Rationing of civilian goods over here is quite severe,' he continued. 'It seems that a bar of soap will get almost anything for you. One lad has a "shack" with company for one bar a week. Most of the boys writing home tell the folks about how severe things are in comparison with the States. Americans still have it very easy by contrast.'

During Johnny's final week in England, they had entertainment at the camp. 'Tonight, as part of the two entertainment features in camp, we had Yehudi Menuhin and his famous violin. I'm not particularly keen on long-haired musicians, so I went to the movies. Saw Joe Browne in *Casanova in Burlesque*. It was very good.'

7

'Too Bad It Had To Be So Short a Time'

Johnny was transferred into the 359th Infantry, part of the 90th Division of the Third Army, which had been activated in Texas in March 1942. The 359th was mostly made up of men from Texas and Oklahoma, and its emblem was a combination of the letters 'T' and 'O', which the men said stood for 'Tough Ombres'. The 359th landed at Utah Beach on D-Day. Officially, the Third Army stayed in Britain, planning to invade at the Pas de Calais. This was a decoy to fool the Germans. General George S. Patton conspicuously remained in Britain, leading this phantom army. As a result, the Germans were deceived long enough to keep vital units in the Calais region, rather than quickly using them to bolster the defences in Normandy.

In the early fighting, the 90th Division did not distinguish itself. General Omar Bradley noted that it 'turned out to be one of the worst-trained to arrive in the ETO [European Theatre of Operation].' The 90th Division was poorly led by Brigadier General Jay W. McKelvie, who had no rapport with his men and was removed after just five days in combat. Major General Eugene

Lundrum replaced him, but he was little better. Described as short, fat and uninspiring, Lundrum could not motivate his troops, because he 'commanded the division from an armchair in a cellar.' He was removed after five weeks. 'The 90th became a "problem" division,' according to General Bradley. 'So exasperating was its performance that at one point the First Army Staff gave up and recommended that we break it up for replacements. Instead, we stayed with the division and in the end the 90th became one of the most outstanding in the European theatre.'

At the end of July, Lieutenant General Raymond McLain took over command of the 90th Division, around the same time that Patton took operational control of the Third Army. Patton was a tough, no-nonsense soldier who thrived on war. He summed up his philosophy as: 'I don't want you sons of bitches to die for your country; I want to send you sons of bitches out to make other sons of bitches die for their country.' By the end of August, the Third Army had driven bridgeheads across to the Seine. Patton had the Germans on the run and he was anxious to press home the advantage, but his petrol supply almost dried up. 'The Third Army had advanced so rapidly, covering such great distances, it had overextended its lines of communication,' Major John H. Cochran of the 359th later wrote.

Between the start of August and the end of the first week in September, the forward headquarters of the Third Army moved nine times, covering 515 miles. After liberating Reims, the 90th Division had hardly enough fuel to keep the field ranges on the kitchen trucks going. Other elements of the Third Army were on the Moselle by 2 September and there was no sign of Germans on the other side. 'Just give me four hundred thousand gallons of petrol and I'll put you inside Germany in two days,' Patton pleaded with General Omar Bradley. 'All I need are those lousy four hundred thousand gallons of petrol to win this goddam war.'

The Allies had advanced much further than they had planned. Prior to the D-Day landing, the aim had been to end the war in 263 days. By 11 September, the Allies were already 233 days ahead of schedule. At that rate, the war should only have had another thirty days to run. Patton was convinced that the Third Army could push into Germany with little difficulty and shorten the war, but Eisenhower and his staff cut off his petrol supplies in order to send it to the forces under Field Marshall Bernard Montgomery to the north. The disorganised Germans were given the opportunity to reorganise on both the Maginot and Siegfried Lines, in preparation for the Allied assault. Had the Third Army not been denied supplies at this vital juncture at the start of September, Patton was convinced that his men would have cut through the Maginot and Siegfried defences at the Saar and gone straight to the Rhine.

It was at this point that Johnny Dwyer joined the 359th Infantry Regiment of the 90th Division. He landed in Normandy in the middle of September 1944. 'I saw such places as Caen and Argentan and the beach on which the invasion started,' he wrote on 11 September. 'The rules of censorship prevent my describing the scenes. But the people seem to move through the ruins with a very detached air. Most of those we see are friendly to us.'

'This area we now occupy was German ground just three weeks ago,' he continued. 'There are very few signs of their occupancy. In fact we have called the GIs' attention to the fact that the Germans kept things pretty good.'

'We just had an interesting talk with a boy about sixteen years old. I was sitting by the road writing when he passed,' Johnny wrote on 14 September. 'I bid him *"Bonsoir"* and he replied "Good evening." I was very much surprised. He is a French boy who studied English at Caen five years ago. Until the invasion by the Allies, he had no chance to use his English. He said that the French knew when and where to expect the Allied bombers and would go to another part of town at night. He said the Germans went out of the town of Le Mans (where he was at the time of invasion) in trucks with big guns, but came back on foot leaning on sticks or carrying clubs. He said, "We laughed behind our windows." He was very intelligent and most interesting.'

'One of the lieutenants (who doesn't know French) managed to buy some eggs,' Johnny continued. 'He had to sit down and cackle and reach under to indicate an egg. But it worked.'

'My mail still hasn't arrived, but when it does I expect to have quite a handful,' he wrote at the start of his second month overseas. 'One of the boys got his the other day – the first since May. He had over eighty letters altogether.' When another got a bundle of letters at the same time, he just opened one on a daily basis, so that he had a new letter each day.

'Along the road near here, we see the people of the

cities making their way back to their homes,' he wrote on 20 September. 'I guess they were hiding in the hills. It's like the pictures we saw when the "Boches" invaded France. Only now everybody is smiling as they walk along with bikes or on big trucks or on foot. People riding bikes with baby carriages for trailers.'

'Today I did quite a bit of walking, looking over my surroundings,' he wrote three days later. 'I talked to a couple of French kids and actually got some information of interest from them. They seem so funny in a way. Driving cows to pasture in old battlefields. Believe it or not, there are "feather merchants" over here too. I bought a fountain pen, a wristwatch and a bottle of White Horse Scotch. My new buddies found me a very welcome person. We finished the Scotch last night at one sitting. And may I remark, everybody has a headache but me. They also liked the American Hershey bars I carried with me.'

On 21 September, Bing Crosby brought his show to the troops. Even though Johnny had seen it on the boat coming over, he took the opportunity to go again. 'It seemed wonderful out here, even seeing it a second time,' he wrote. 'Except for the nurses they'd seen on their trips to hospital (at which time they also saw the Red Cross), the girls on the programme were the only American girls these fellows have seen in a long time. Those girls will never be so popular again anywhere.'

'Yesterday there were some kids hanging around our kitchen,' he wrote on 26 September. 'They seemed to be quite young. One was actually about seven. The sister looks about twelve, but was seventeen. A girl passed by who looked twenty. She was actually in her thirties. Since that incident, the men have been very careful about the "girls" they try to date. They can't seem to judge age correctly. We have a few who can speak some French and a few others who would get along anywhere. It's fun to watch the way they all get along together.'

'The war seems to be going pretty well, from all reports,' he wrote in the same letter. 'The Germans seem to be holding out in certain localities. They are usually fanatics of some sort. I imagine they are bucking for Wehrmacht commissions. In the next German war they will be running things.'

'Whoever said this is "sunny France" was nuts,' he wrote on 2 October. 'When the sun shines we have hail instead of rain and it gets cold. Right now I have a blanket over my feet and legs. As I have nothing but a K-ration box to lean on right now, this will be sort of rough.'

'This is a noisy place sometimes,' he continued. That was a subtle way of indicating that there was heavy shelling. 'I don't tell you very much of what's going on, for obvious reasons. I don't want you to build up any stories I tell, so I won't tell you about anything that won't be in the papers. I don't want you worrying. My home is a hole two feet wide and about five feet long and four feet deep. I'm behind a low bank (hedgerow) on top of a hill. My roof is two shelter halves. I have two blankets with me, both muddy – as I am myself. Also my field coat (thank God). My sewed-on insignia is pretty muddy. My hands and face (except for my long beard) are the same colour as my field jacket, shoes, pants and gloves – mud. It's like the rainy days in Carolina, only colder.

'Most of my daylight hours are spent censoring mail.

There's one kid who can reach my hole without walking too far. He has a pad of paper and a pack of envelopes and he keeps me busy. There's another screwball who thinks his wife in unfaithful to him. He writes her four or five V-mails a day. The way things look right now makes me wonder about everything. The war should be over soon, or else it is due to last for a good while.'

Each of the men was issued with a small shovel with a fold-down head that they carried attached to their cartridge belt. They did three kinds of digging – a slit trench, a foxhole or a bunker. A slit trench was roughly six feet long by two feet wide, and about a foot deep. It provided some protection against artillery, mortar or small-arms fire but was of little use in the event of the position being run over by a tank. A foxhole, on the other hand, was about six feet deep and was normally used for two men. It provided more protection against tanks, but it was necessary for someone to be on watch at all times in a two-man foxhole. As a result, they had to take turns in two- to three-hour watches a couple of times a night. A bunker was larger and a more permanent than either a slit trench or a foxhole, and was often roofed over. It usually accommodated three or more men, and the number of men in the bunker usually governed the amount of sleep that a soldier got at night. Nobody got a full night's sleep while on the line, but it was best if there were three or four to share the watch duties.

'Today I am not sitting in a muddy hole – for a little change,' he wrote on 4 October. 'We are resting a while in a grove of fir trees. Of course we have our holes dug and ready in case anything should happen. Our own artillery keeps us company with its banging and whistling. We like its sound, though. My platoon sergeant and I have a very good hole with a wooden roof and a shelter tent pitched over the door. We have straw on the bottom and five blankets. So we are quite comfortable. Yesterday I didn't have a chance to write because I spent the whole day censoring the platoon mail. And there was plenty. One dodo wrote five letters to his wife – all the same line of drivel and impossible to read. I figure if I can't dope it out, Jerry can't either, so I let it go.

'We were busy last night for half the night, so I didn't try to write in the tent by flash- or candle-light. While we were working (fatigue detail) (I mean it – no fighting) we took a prisoner. He walked right up to us with his hands on his head. He was a kid eighteen years old and scared sh—less, as the GI Joes say. He had no weapon of any kind. That was my first chance to try my German. He must have been sneaking through for quite a while, because he was weak and frightened. I guess he didn't want to show up right in front where everybody is jumpy. The boys had me asking him questions like "How's the Führer?" and "Where does your mother live?", "Where's the *Luftwaffe?*", etc. He answered quickly and willingly: *"Ich weiss nichts"* – "I don't know."

'It is quite chilly here now, although today we have some sunshine. In a little while the birdmen will be out raising hell in the neighborhood. I still need a shave and a good washing, but I'm going to pass both up, because the dirtier I look, the more GI I look – which is good over here. You'll have to re-educate me when I get home. I wipe my fingers on my pants and everything now. Reading other people's mail sort of inhibits me. I'd like to pour my heart out to you, but it sounds so unoriginal. You know I love you more than the whole world and that all I look for out of life is to be with you for a chance to make you happy. I haven't been through hell like some of my buddies, but I'm paying a little for our future now by being so far away from you. Not hearing from anybody is the worst of it all.'

In his first six weeks at the front, Johnny had had only one letter from home, as his mail had not caught up with him yet. The Germans were still so disorganised that there was no real front line for a time. When either side went out on patrol at night, they would penetrate enemy lines and pass within earshot of each other. 'I've heard the Jerries talking amongst themselves,' Johnny wrote on 4 October. 'I hope you are praying for the end of the war. I don't think it should last till after this month. If the Siegfried Line cracks, as we hope, I think it will be over here. I'd sure like to get back to being a chemist again for a while, for a change. Even at that pay. I'd sure agitate for more after all this discomfort.'

Knowing that Johnny had still not got his mail when he went to France, Margaret reasoned that he would get mail addressed to his new address before the other mail caught up with him, so she wrote a letter bringing him up to date with all that had happened since he'd left in August. She had actually informed him in a letter written on 19 August that she had found a new apartment in Woodside in Queens, New York. As she had thought, Margaret's first letter to his new address reached him before any of the other mail. In this letter she described the hunt for somewhere to live and the six-room apartment she found in the upstairs of a two-apartment house.

The neighbours downstairs were an Irish couple from County Galway who had their six American-born children. Jim Philbin, a senior detective in the New York Police Department, was from Gortnamona. A big, bluff, outspoken Irishman, he was as proud of his Irishness and his Galway heritage as he was of his growing family, the youngest of whom was just over a year older than Ryle. The house had a fenced-in backyard, so Margaret was able to leave the baby there 'from dawn to dusk'. She told Johnny about her purchase of a car seat for Ryle, as well as a crib, which she described as 'the joy of his life. First of all, he can get on his hands and knees and crawl all about the crib. You never know where you will find him. He is rather a remarkable baby. He doesn't sit up yet – at least not very well – but can crawl. Then, too, he has a high chair and of course "Nosy" is in seventh heaven when he can be in the middle of things.

'If you thought he ate like a chow hound before, you should see your son now,' she continued. 'Big bowls of cereal, bananas, meat and vegetables (the strained kind), soup and potatoes. To top that, he has four eight-ounce bottles of milk a day and finishes every bit of them. I am enclosing some snaps of him and I had his picture taken yesterday.' No doubt the contents of this letter were similar to what many young mothers sent to their husbands overseas.

'Then item two,' she went on, 'you will have a little thumperess in March. Nice work, my boy.' This was the news that she was pregnant with their second child.

'All I can write about is how excited I am about the news about Thumper (should we have a new name?), but

I have a guilty-worried feeling,' he wrote back. 'After all, two babies in one year will sure be a strain on you. I sure do hope you take care of yourself and our family. If anything should happen to you, there'll be one damn fool soldier over here instead of a conservative, careful officer.'

Thereafter, Johnny frequently wrote his letters on the back of Margaret's letters. 'I am writing this on your letters so that we can save them for Ryle to know what we were doing and thinking during these unusual days,' he explained. 'I think some of them will give him something to think about, don't you? I spend about half my time trying to figure out a way to beat the next draft for a certain young man of our acquaintance. I could kick myself when I think about some of the ways I had of getting out of this myself – and passed up. Well, when it's over we can say we did our part and made our sacrifice for what we hold dear.'

On 8 October, Johnny's father telephoned Margaret in a state of high excitement. Johnny's photograph was on the front page of the *New York Herald Tribune* with a group of soldiers who were gathered around a radio in Lorraine, listening to a World Series baseball game from St Louis. The next day, the same photograph was on the front page of the *New York Times*. 'Today was one of those miserable days with lots of mist, rain and clouds,' Johnny wrote on 12 October. 'We don't have much other trouble, except our French allies sticking their heads out too far and drawing Jerry fire. They show themselves too much – they are very brave and a little foolhardy. Thank the Lord – they take most of the night patrols around here.'

'I'd like to tell you about a couple of adventures I've

had in the last couple of days,' he wrote on 15 October. 'One night I went out on a listening patrol with three of my men. Before we'd done twenty-five yards, a Jerry patrol passed behind us. Well, you can imagine how surprised we were. Anyway, we had to go on. Well, we passed at least twenty of the s–o–b–s, did our job and returned.'

'Tonight I'm sitting in the company command post,' he continued. 'Everybody has exhausted their jokes and the men have now reached the stage where they will bet on anything. First they bet on when the phone would ring. Next, on when a certain man would move in his sleep. Now they are betting on when the next artillery barrage will be fired.'

'Talking about the end of the war,' he wrote on 20 October, 'I sincerely hope you and all your friends are shunning the black market where gasoline in particular is concerned. That particular fluid might have ended the war one or two months ago if it had been over here when it was called for. Maybe the black market had nothing to do with it, but I believe it probably had a lot to do with it.' The Americans had run out of petrol on the ground and were now bogged down, as they could not continue to harry the Germans. 'I am in my little old foxhole again,' he continued. 'And you can probably judge that the weather has been somewhat miserable for over a week. Also our Jerry "friends" are posing incongruities for us. Sort of now you see them, now you don't. Yesterday and today we heard them whistling by, but today we have some clear weather and the old throttle-jockies are on the beam. Last night we had a lot of bombers fly over. It must scare the hell out of the Germans to hear them.

117

The whole sky seems to roar in one continuous hum, all moving eastward. It's an unforgettable experience which leaves a wonderful sense of security.'

'The war part of this thing eventually loses its aspect of terror which most people experience at first. It soon becomes a game of skill and a battle of wits,' he continued. 'We have the most players and best equipment, and the players put more into playing the game. We sit here and try to guess from where the few Jerry shells do come, and count the seconds they are in the air to judge the range. With enough of us doing it, we locate their guns and – kaput – as the Frenchmen say. The men sometimes bet on whether or not they'll have to dive within a certain period of time. GIs are the same everywhere. Did I tell you about going to Mass and Communion last Sunday?' he went on. 'We have a swell chaplain. Even the Jews and Baptists go to mass when they get a chance. Remember that quotation: "There are no atheists in foxholes." That's the absolute truth.'

The following week, he got a four-day break from the front. This meant that he could take his shoes off at night, undress and sleep between sheets. 'There's a lot to be said for that,' he wrote on 30 October. 'You know, I guess that we don't have dry-cleaning facilities handy. In fact, even laundry isn't convenient. It's cold enough here that we don't sweat, and so we have mostly the outside dirt to worry about. My outside trousers and field jacket take a beating, you can guess. Between the mud and the charcoal and the black from my canteen cup, the ensemble is not particularly beautiful. However, that makes me blend with the background better. You know me. I never went for flashy clothes much. I guess it sounds silly, but one of my first purchases after the war is going to be a tuxedo. Does that agree with you? Then we can dress for dinner and so on in proper style.

'To get back to the rest we had – we had hot meals the whole time, just what they consisted of is immaterial except for the fresh pork. Some very small tiny little pigs were suspected of harbouring Nazi tendencies and ideas, so they were accidentally disposed of when the "guard" thought they were a patrol trying to pass our wire. What a fate – to become fresh sausage! So none of us has had normal digestion since.'

'During the day I talked to a lot of the kids, trying my little French on them,' he continued. 'One little girl offered me a holy picture. I gave her a piece of gum. Right away I was offered a handful of pictures – for gum, of course. *"Un cigarette pour papa, bon-bon pour mama, et choog gum pour moi!"* They chant it everywhere. Sometimes one meets a little fellow with a little girl who can just barely walk: *"Avez-vous bon-bon pour ma petite soeur?"* They are cute little monkeys.

'Our little holiday over, we returned to our main business. There's a part of France that I know better than I know any part of the USA. And I don't like my neighbours, believe me. They aren't nice people – they should happen to Hitler.'

'My platoon command post tonight smells like a short-order restaurant,' he concluded his letter of 30 October 1944. 'We have been French-frying potatoes. The boys admit that my French fries are better than their "home" fries. We are trying the spuds as a change from the GI diet. Another change we tried is making a jam or conserve out of "nut and fruit" bar from K-ration. It's very good.

I've been drinking my lemonade daily too to ward off cold – that supplies vitamin C.

'Well, darling, this letter has covered four hours of the busiest night I've had so far. I've been using three phones, and I'm worrying about two patrols and one special outpost, but I think I'll knock off for the night right now.' He did not mention that the officers had been called back to hear a pep talk from General George Patton. Major General James A. Van Fleet had replaced General McLain as commanding officer of the 90th Division in late October. The Third Army was about to embark on its third campaign since the start of August. This time their aim was to seize the city of Metz, which had never been seized by any enemy in an attack since 415 AD. Many people therefore considered it to be an impregnable fortress. Its defences consisted of a network of two dozen forts built in two tiers around Metz and in a line between the city and Thionville.

'We are pretty busy these days,' Johnny wrote on 6 November. 'Of course I can't tell you what we are doing. It's interesting, though, and anything but monotonous.' They were making final preparations for the assault on Metz. He enclosed a cartoon from *Stars and Stripes* that 'struck me so funny,' he explained. 'A lot of the boys sent it to their girlfriends with all kinds of warnings. During the last couple of nights, there have been some dances in the town where we are billeted. And the same birds who are sending warnings to their wives are raising all kinds of hell in the neighbourhood. I haven't gone to any of the dances myself.

'Yesterday we had an unusual treat. We were given an issue of captured liquor. There was wine of a rather weak (to me) variety, some vermouth, which one of the boys said was of the best prewar variety in France, and some brandy. The latter was superb. I had ten bottles all told. So I took my platoon headquarters and put one man from it into each squad, and my platoon sergeant, platoon guide and myself had one bottle of brandy. The rest we split three ways, and everybody was happy. The effect of the brandy wore off after a couple of hours, though, and I went to work censoring mail. I was too tired to finish or write to you last night. I hope you'll forgive me.

'The men are getting rest and exercise,' he continued. 'Ordinarily they don't get much exercise, but don't get continuous sleep either. I have a blanket-lined sleeping bag. It has a water-resistant cloth cover over it. The combination is very good. We are able to undress at night, so the sleeping bag is swell. Incidentally, I still have – but don't use – the sheets and pillowcases. I'm saving them for after the war. A lot of us still hope that will take place before Christmas. There's no hope of being home by then, though – much as we'd like it. All my buddies in the South Pacific seem to be having a time with tropical diseases. That was the thing I disliked most about that area. It seemed to me to be too much against a man. Has anyone heard from Harry Hoffman? He was so damn anxious to get into combat. I wonder if he's still so crazy about it.' In the next four weeks, the Third Army would liberate some 1,600 square miles of territory, which included 873 towns. In the process, the Americans took 30,000 prisoners and killed or wounded 88,000 Germans, suffering some 23,000 casualties in the process.

8

Johnny, We Hardly Knew You

The attack on Metz began on 8 November 1944. The main effort had been assigned to the 90th Division. Patton had ordered it to move to the Cattenom Forest and attack across the Moselle through the fortified Koenigsmacher area and the Maginot Line. The Americans attacked without air support because the planes could not get up in the bad weather. The 359th crossed the Moselle near Thionville in the early hours of 9 November. 'I suppose by this time the story of the Koenigsmacher bridgehead over the Moselle river is now cold in the home news-papers,' he wrote some weeks later. 'Anyway, it is cold enough now to tell you that I was in on that. We were supposed to be in the second wave, but somehow the first wave got to the wrong place on the river and your hubby and his platoon found three empty boats and got across the river. The attack on a river line, by the way, is considered the most difficult and dangerous military operation. It so happened after I got across that we were about a half a mile from where we belonged because of the heavy current and so on. It was the worst river conditions in thirty years. We went upstream to where we should have been, and then started into Jerryland. We passed two towns and reached our objective – a woods – and waited for the rest of the company. For us it was a dry run – like manoeuvres. Some of the others didn't do as well. There is more to the story, but I'll tell you all about that when I come home. There were the nights without blankets and eating cabbage and raw potatoes and so on – R-R-R-Rough.'

On 12 November the Germans counter-attacked. The 359th came under very heavy fire and was driven from the town of Kerling. At one point it looked like they might be overrun, but for the phenomenal bravery of one man, Sergeant Forrest E. Everhart, who was in charge of a small heavy-weapons platoon. As the Germans threatened to overrun Everhart's machine-gun nest, which was the last one left, he directed his one remaining gunner to direct furious fire at the advancing Germans and he then ran four hundred yards through a hail of bullets to a position from which he exchanged hand grenades with the enemy for about fifteen minutes before the Germans withdrew, leaving some thirty dead troops.

Everhart then ran to another position and directed his machine-gun crew to fire at a further group of advancing Germans. Amid a hail of mortar fire, Everhart closed in on the Germans and showered them with grenades. After about thirty minutes, the Germans withdrew, leaving a further twenty dead. He had delayed the German advance long enough for help to arrive, and the German assault was routed.

'We had a mighty rugged week without blankets for a while and without much to eat either,' Johnny wrote on

17 November. 'In spite of it all, we are very happy at what we've done.' Patton visited the scene and was thrilled with what he found. 'I have never seen so many dead Germans in one place in my life,' he remarked. 'They extended for a distance of about a mile, shoulder to shoulder.' In all, more than two hundred Germans were killed and a further hundred and fifty were taken prisoner in the area west of Kerling. 'We've been having a regular picnic for two or three days,' Johnny wrote on 20 November 1944. 'Of course the Jerry B-s may change that at any time, but we're enjoying the chase tremendously. We "liberated" several populated places, as the communiqués say. Darling, it is a terrific thrill to ride or walk into a town alone or with two or three GI Joes (beards and all), to find maybe one brave old man waiting to greet you. A friendly *"Bonjour, papa"* gets you a big smile and a handshake and a hug and shouts of, *"Les Americains!"* The houses empty – the street fills with people so happy they jump and laugh like children. They laugh and cry and simply lose all control of themselves in their emotion. You've seen children tremble with excitement at the prospect of a gift or candy – just picture grown people that excited.

'Our company commander is a real wag,' he continued. 'At one place he came up to me and said I should climb on the fender of the jeep and we'd liberate the next place alone. He said it would look good that way in the local paper – if they had a photographer. So he and I and the driver went in alone. It's really a funny thing to watch. Sometimes we do it kinda noisy like with airplanes and tanks and shootin'. So far – thank God – I haven't lost a man in combat, even wounded. Of course, the lad who fell into a cellar and bruised his knee, and the one who got diarrhoea too bad for our trouser supply aren't combat casualties.

'The other day we became separated from the company for twenty-four hours. During that time our orders changed, to shorten the distance we were to go. We slept on the new objective and then pushed on to the old one, which was considered too hard to take without tanks. We were there four hours before we got in touch again and were called back. We were the "celebrated lost platoon" who took the regimental objective alone. All of which shows – your prayers are working wonders. Yesterday we had what looked like a "dry run" as we approached a certain town. Just as we were about to strike it, a bunch of P 47 started to strafe it. We pushed right in anyway, and I set up my platoon to block a certain road. One squad I detailed to search some houses, and my headquarters to follow me into the centre of town, where I'd meet the chief. Well, gawd-almighty, you shoulda heard the noise and seen the running about. About seventy Jerries surrendered to us in one end of town while one intoxicated soul decided to fight it out in another part of town. When things quieted down, we had destroyed several trucks and armoured vehicles and captured quite a bit of booty. I made sure the men wouldn't take pictures, rings or any of that sort of things from the prisoners.'

'Still in France,' he wrote on 24 November 1944: 'Yesterday and today I've been enjoying a wonderful break. Someone had to go to a rest area behind the active front. We aren't very far back, but we can't hear guns, and we don't have to stay awake nights sweating out counter-attacks. It's a real rest, and I'm certainly glad to be here. We left the company yesterday morning at 7.15 and drove back over the same road that my platoon "drove" through. I left a little bit pleased to note that my boys had opened the main drag. When we got here, we were oriented and then we had chow-down. Just cold cuts. In the afternoon we had showers and rest and free beer. Supper was Thanksgiving dinner. Yes, darling, it was an American Thanksgiving with turkey and all. The real thrill of the evening was unlimited ice cream. I forgot to tell you we had Mass at four and I went to Communion. We all agreed with the chaplain that we had much to be thankful for. Well, all the boys on the front in this sector have enjoyed their Thanksgiving turkey, either at rest camp or on the line.'

That night they had an army show 'with a dancer and a singer and a magician and a girl who was involved in some slapstick,' he continued. 'After the show we sat and did a post-mortem or Monday-morning quarterbacking of the past campaign. There are seven of us from 359th in two rooms. We didn't know each other yesterday. Now we are well acquainted. The common bond between soldiers of one unit is very strong. Some of these boys were in on the D-Day adventure and have stories to tell.

'This morning we had a plentiful breakfast of hot cakes,' he continued. 'This required waiting out a long line. Next we got into the line before the Red Cross club mobile for doughnuts and coffee. That was sure good too, believe me. Doughnuts are really American as the flag. Hearing the voices of American girls is a pleasure too, even though most

of the men only hear, "Hand your cup up here, soldier." We had a typical ration lunch of corned-beef hash, lima beans, potatoes and cabbage – the latter being a novelty on our menu. This afternoon we attended a movie and again tonight two more. One was Lana Turner in *Marriage Is a Private Affair*. The baby in that was just like Ryle was when he was at two or three months. Tomorrow morning we return to our outfits. We don't know what's ahead, but you can bet it's not good for our enemy.'

His early mail had taken so long to reach him that Margaret sent his Christmas mail early and he received it during this break, so he took the opportunity to write a number of Christmas cards. The one to Margaret was written on 23 November: 'Dearest Margaret, it seems awfully early to be writing Christmas cards – I have already received yours, and Ryle and "Thumperess", and I sure wish I could be with you for a Merry Christmas. With the news as good as it is according to the papers, we ought not be around here too much longer, and God willing we'll be together next Christmas. All my love is yours, darling, John.'

The next day he wrote a card to Ryle:

The letter on p.129 was on the back of this ca

Margaret and Johnny en route to California, 1943

Members of Johnny's regiment, the 359th Infantry, about to go on leave (and thankful for a chance to escape the mud at the front)

The 90th infantry division's camp close to the front line

American soldiers on the road to Metz

Americans cluster around a radio to hear a world series game as one keeps score on a captured pillbox

This picture appeared on the front page of the *New York Herald Tribune* on 9 October 1944 (and of the *New York Times* the following day). Johnny Dwyer is third from the left, behind the truck.

Bob Hope and Francis Langford, 1942

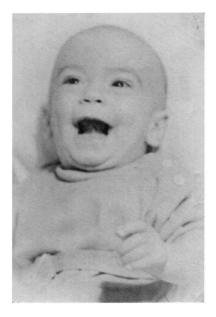

The laughing baby: 'Ryle looked like a little peanut,' Margaret said.

Therese with Ryle on pony. Johnny referred to both of these photos in his letters.

Margaret's classmate Judith Tuvim, who won the Oscar for Best Actress for her role in *Born Yesterday* (1950) under the stage name Judy Holliday, with Broderick Crawford

Margaret with Ryle (left) and Sean posing
for a passport photograph, 1948

Sean (left) and Ryle make their First Communion, 1951,
with, from left, Margaret, Mary Harrigan and Therese Harrigan

Mary Harrigan, Sean, Margaret Furlong, Margaret and Ryle, 1962

Brendan O'Reilly introduces the 1973 Rose of Tralee, Veronica McCambridge, at the Ashe Memorial Hall. With them are Margaret, the Festival president, and Denis Reen, its chairman.

'A rose is a rose is a rose':
Margaret in 1971

The Festival Committee on the steps of the Ashe Memorial Hall.
From left: Bob Cosgrave, Ted Keane, Dorothy Chard, Nancy Caball,
Denis Reen, Margaret, Matt Walsh and Dick O'Sullivan.

Margaret being presented with honorary citizenship of Tralee by Norma Foley, chairperson of Tralee UDC. On the right is Noreen Cassidy, chief executive of the Rose of Tralee Festival.

From left: Noreen Cassidy, former Rose of Tralee presenter Gay Byrne and Margaret

2 t Nov. 44
France

My Dear Son

I will be a long time till Christmas and a long time till you will understand where your Daddy is now. This picture will give you an idea of how my feelings are for little boys. I sure do miss you and wish I could be with you when you get this card. Of course your daddy looks different with beard and mud and head net and tommy gun, but we all sure do want to get home to our own boys & girls — love
your dad

This letter was on the back of the card on p.128

The 359th Infantry crossed the Saar river into Germany proper the following day. 'Since the shortest way to New York is by way of Germany, we are all trying like hell to go that way,' he wrote from 'Somewhere in Germany' on 27 November 1944. 'Walking into Germany was quite an experience,' he explained the following week. 'Naturally we were greeted by cheering throngs and everybody decked in holiday garb, throwing flower pots and mortar shells and so on. Literally a celebration with fireworks. We got started a couple of days ago, and while the Germans don't like it so much, we are celebrating the trip homeward (in the future) with considerable fireworks right now.

'My first impression of the German people (within walking distance of French people) is that they are so much cleaner and, frankly, more advanced than those we just passed. So far we haven't had to pass through a barn or over a four-foot-high dung-heap to get into the home part of the houses. Everything is newer-looking and in better condition. There are servants in every house. These servants are of various nationalities. In one home we encountered a young Ukrainian girl. Her brother was in another home in the town. The relationship in the house in each case was very familiar, i.e. a man and his mother calling the servant girl "sister" and "daughter" respectively. In other words, she wasn't a slave exactly. It's a funny sort of war.

'This letter is written with considerable effort,' he continued. 'It is cold and frosty and it's now 2.30 PM. The sun gets a little way above the horizon in the morning and then just swings around until sunset. As I sit here, I think about how nice it is in New York, where it's always

130

a beautiful day – because you're there. My little home right now is a hole two and a half feet deep and just wide enough and long enough for me and one of my runners to sleep in. We've got the earth mounded around the hole and a pup tent pitched over it. I got some straw for the bottom, which just about makes it perfect for the job. Fortunately it is a dry spot, although there is a stream about ten feet away. I have a sleeping bag as well as three blankets. We use one blanket and a rain cape underneath, and two blankets over us. That's a pretty comfortable bed.

'Did you see the movie *The Eager Years?* In that, a soldier comes home after a year and a half overseas. He gets a blanket from the closet (a wedding gift) and sleeps on the floor because he isn't used to springs and a mattress after sleeping on the ground. Well, to make some postwar plans – I'm not going to sleep on the ground the first night home – or any night. I'd be so glad to be near you again that I'd stay awake willingly to be near you. Another thing I'm looking forward to – a good dinner with you – this for me and whatever your heart desires for you: shrimp salad – your way, steak medium with mushrooms, French fries as Mother D. makes them, fresh peas – your way, some good hot coffee or tea, chocolate fudge layer cake for dessert and some good wine. Not very well balanced probably, but it's a dream anyway.'

'There isn't much news to write about,' Johnny wrote from Germany on 9 December. 'We have with us as usual the rain, the Krauts and good old K-ration. We are out in the woods again, thank goodness, and now that the smell of manure piles is remote, our digestive systems are getting back in shape. It is beginning to worry me – must I always live in the woods? Our first sergeant is getting a furlough to the States to find out if we can ever live decently again. I've told him to call on you for a home-cooked meal when he gets to New York.'

Johnny would be out of the woods the following week, but he obviously found little comfort in a captured German pillbox on the Siegfried Line. 'It's been rough here for the last week,' he wrote on 17 December. 'We have been in a Siegfried Line pillbox most of the time. We go out for fresh air and sunshine when there isn't too much steel around. At the moment I am inside and still wearing my helmet. Rough. I haven't written before because the return transportation has been strictly priority. The sun is shining and the throttle-jockeys are up – thank God. I hope they do us some good. There are some Jerry big guns out there that I have a particular hate for. The night I came across I changed one Jerry's mind with my pistol – he had a bag of grenades. If I catch up with this particular gun crew, I'll . . . Business is picking up, so I'll close now and get out where I can see. I'll write more tonight.'

'Tonight is one of those nights we sweat out,' he continued later. 'It's dark enough to hide, and yet bright enough to move about in. We have patrols out, so we aren't throwing anything. Jerry isn't either, so we infer that he's snooping too. So we sweat it out. The air corps gave us a good show this afternoon. And our cubs came out right over us. So the boys had a fairly good afternoon. The Jerry artillery and mortars are afraid of our cubs. They don't use them themselves or we would have headaches.

132

'A week in a pillbox is enough to drive a person a little wacky. I've been doing all sorts of things to keep my mind occupied. I was amazed to learn that so much of my mail is examined and so little cut out. A darn sight more than I can tell you goes into the newspapers. Tomorrow I'm going to find a puddle of water and wash. I'm so dirty now I can't stand myself any more. Washing usually makes one so darn cold that it isn't worth it except when you're handling food. However, I'm still disgustingly healthy. Jerry just pasted us with a few big ones, so believe it or not, we feel better. Quiet is so unusual that we distrust it. It's only one week till Christmas. We wonder how it will be. Well, I wish it could be a peaceful and happy one for us all. We don't intend to let Jerry have much quiet, because he certainly won't give us any.'

'We are looking for a field day of Jerry shooting in the near future, and probably it will help end the war,' he wrote from 'Somewhere in Germany' on 19 December. 'I received the picture of Ryle on a pony tonight. It's a riot. He's the most wonderful morale-booster. I get a big lift when I see the serious little face. The laughing picture I carry in my pocket – cut down, of course. I've shown that one to everybody around here and, believe me, it helps everyone. I shaved today. I have a beautiful wide mustache to the side of my cheeks. I am going to look like a Russian – scare hell out of the Jerries.'

To the north, the Germans had already launched their counter-offensive in the Ardennes in what became known as the Battle of the Bulge. The battle got its name from the bulge created in the Allied lines as the Germans recaptured ground as far as Bastogne in Belgium. In fact, they surrounded Bastogne and demanded that the American forces surrender. The general in charge responded with one word: 'Nuts.' One of his troops is reported to have said, 'The Germans have us surrounded, the poor bastards.' Bastogne held out until it was relieved by Patton's Third Army.

The 359th was withdrawn from the pillboxes they had been occupying on the other side of the Saar river on 22 December. Patton visited the front and wanted to go down to the river to observe it. 'He went into one of the houses on our side of the river and was looking out of a second-storey window when the Germans began mortaring the area,' Lieutenant Colonel Orwin Talbott recalled. 'Afterwards the press hounded us as to Patton's reaction. We told them the truth. His immortal words were, "Where the hell is my helmet?"'

Johnny's next letter was written on Christmas Day, on the back of Margaret's letter of three weeks earlier. 'Today was a better Xmas than I expected it would be. I am in a town again working like I did when Colonel Culp had me with him – blast him anyway. It's quite safe here, so just rest easy about me . . . This morning at noon I went to Mass and Communion in the town church. Our chaplain said Mass. I prayed to God for a speedy end to the war, and a quick return to my little family. I thanked Him for taking such good care of us. During the last three weeks I've seen a lot of people decide there is a God and start praying. I've been through some pretty rugged living and saw some sudden things happen. Somehow I never doubted that I'd be writing to you on Christmas Day, but them German fellers can sure worry a person sometimes.

Do you know what kind of people I associate with? The Catholic chaplain was the Rev Donald J. Murphy, who was highly respected by the men. "I'd sure like to see about 400,000 Germans go to heaven for Christmas," Father Murphy remarked the previous night. His sentiments were echoed in different degrees by everyone present. We had an unusual breakfast – hot-cakes and fresh eggs. We had one other meal – dinner: nearly two pounds of turkey per man. With dressing, asparagus, mashed potatoes, gravy, apples, nuts, candy and iced cake. Also snow on the ground. I still don't use an overcoat – nor my trench coat. Of course we all have colds.'

'We are having good hot cooked meals every day now, but it's been so long since we ate them regularly that now we all have K-ration stomach,' Johnny wrote on 30 December 1944. 'I can't eat much of anything at mealtime. We've all got colds, but the morale of the troops is wonderful. We are all looking forward to seeing Jerry take a good lacing real soon. The 90th Division was called on to relieve Bastogne. They had to make their way under arctic conditions with heavy snow on the ground and temperatures plummeting below zero Fahrenheit. On his way to Arlon on 6 January, Patton passed through the rear of the 90th Division as it was going into battle. The men had been in their trucks for some time in freezing conditions. It was actually –21 degrees Celsius. More men were disabled by frostbite than by the enemy in the arctic conditions. On one side of the road there was a column of ambulances returning with wounded. It was a grim war scene, but when the men spotted Patton in his jeep they jumped to their feet and cheered him. "It was the most moving experience of my life," Patton wrote. "The knowledge of what the ambulances contained made it still more poignant."'

'Right now I haven't much to write,' Johnny wrote to Margaret that day. 'We are busy as usual – being the best division in the army. Read about us! I'll write more when I get a chance.' The 90th Division launched an offensive on 9 January; the 359th captured Nothum. The next day, Patton visited the 90th Division headquarters and was informed that the 359th had already achieved its ultimate objective, a crossroads between Bastogne and Wiltz. It was only after Patton departed that someone realised he had been misinformed. On learning of the mistake, Major General James A. Van Fleet, the commanding officer of the 90th Division, felt he had two options: to tell Patton he had been misinformed, or to seize the objective that night. Rather than tell Patton, he issued a surprise order for the 359th to launch a night attack. Lieutenant Colonel J. F. 'Foxhole' Smith called his officers together under the canvas of one of his trucks, using a torch to illuminate a map. 'I have been ordered to be on that hill to our front at daylight, and I damn well don't intend to be there by myself,' Smith said.

The plan was for the 3rd Battalion of the 359th to move from a ravine that it was holding to a road, where it would meet the 2nd Battalion, and they would then advance together into a column of files on either side of the snow-covered road. The tanks, tank destroyers and other supporting vehicles were to follow them. 'They moved out around twenty-three hundred hours with everyone moving as quietly as possible,' Lieutenant

Colonel Orwin Talbott recalled. 'It was five degrees below zero. The few Germans found were inside the occasional farmhouse or huddled deep in their foxholes, trying to keep from freezing to death. Complete surprise was obtained. Despite the cold, the battalions were like a hot knife passing through butter.'

'Since resistance had been so dogged and fierce during the day,' Major John H. Cochran recalled, 'we believed the end was at hand. How could anyone survive this night? We would be marching to our certain destruction! What happened to the Germans, we never found out. As we moved through their positions, we could hear them talking on either side of the road. I don't know if they knew we were moving through them and didn't fire, mistook us for another German unit, or plain let their guard down and didn't see us. The road turned out to be a boundary line between their units, and that is always a weak point.

'It was difficult to believe what was happening,' Cochran continued. 'Were we so bold, or were the Germans in shock? We kept moving, waiting for the inevitable to happen. These were the ones who had stopped us in the afternoon and inflicted several casualties on us. They were now sitting on each side of the road and not firing a shot.' After about three miles, they came to a house that contained a German headquarters. A German captain managed to make it into the woods, but he must have assumed that it was just a raiding party or a patrol that was attacking, because he circled back to the road and ran into the side of the column. 'That was the end of his story,' according to Corcoran.

By daybreak, the 90th Division was in a commanding position on top of the hill where Smith had said he didn't intend to be alone. 'The Germans attempted to pull out, and when they did, we opened up with all we had available,' Cochran stated. 'We inflicted many casualties and caused much damage to equipment. Some of it was horse-drawn. The horses never pulled equipment again. It did not take long to render this large unit completely ineffective.' The official US Army history of the battle, written after the war, stated that the German 5th Parachute Division was 'destroyed' in this action. It was 'the only German unit of such large size destroyed in the Battle of the Bulge,' according to that history.

'Tell Dad and everyone that I am OK and very busy,' Johnny Dwyer wrote to Margaret on 15 January. 'You may have heard the radio broadcast about what we did about four days ago. Wherever we go, we bust up a lot of very nice Nazi plans. I got another compass and a new kind of pocket knife. A shell fragment broke up my good field glasses. We captured a Jerry captain and his dugout. Also his last bottle of Cognac, and maps and a pistol and so on.

'There is snow and cold everywhere,' he continued. 'I have a cold, as does everybody, but no frostbite, thank goodness. Right now Jerry is cold and hungry – more than we are – so we are pushing him right back to Germany . . . ' There was not much time for writing.

'I hope we sit still long enough for me to finish this letter to you,' Johnny wrote from 'Somewhere in Luxembourg' on 23 January. 'I started one yesterday, and before

I could finish it we moved two towns closer to Germany. The news just now is all good from over here, I rather imagine. The old-timers say we are going like we did in the breakthrough last summer. Did you read about how we walked through the German lines early one morning for a distance of about a mile and a half? We completely upset him.'

That night, Johnny wrote another letter, this time on captured German paper: 'Since we haven't moved, I can write again and tell you that I haven't forgotten what today means in our lives. It was 23 January 1939 that I met you at the Coelos apartment in Brooklyn. That was probably the luckiest day in my life. I'll never forget, 'cause that was the day I met the most wonderful girl in the world. I love her more than all the world.

'Today I received three letters from you, sweetie,' he continued. 'They were from 25 Dec, 1 Jan and 3 Jan, all postmarked 3 Jan. With Xmas mail the way it was, I guess that's what caused the delay. After several days without mail, we were sure glad to get some today. Well, sweetie, I'll close this letter and write again as soon as possible.'

'Myself and a few of the boys have come back here to a little town for a break of two days,' he wrote from a 'Rest Area in Belgium' on 28 January. 'We are free to wander about and talk to people and so on. There are supposed to be movies and dances and Red Cross trucks. Today I did some shopping for something for you. I'll send the souvenir home when I get a chance. I am well and will write more tomorrow.'

He was 'Back in Luxembourg again' when he wrote

the following day. 'My rest was cut short by a day and I'm back at the company. I did sleep in a hotel for a night – between sheets. The rest camp was overcrowded and so officers were put in a hotel in town. It reminded me of the Cardinal except that there was no heat. I tried my French and German on the Belgians, to very good effect. I bought a pie to take to the movies (so did about twenty-five more of us). I got you a pair of *boucles d'oreilles* and a brooch. We also toured the town's base trying the watered Cognac at about 65¢ a shot – talk about inflation. The pie was about 50¢. But the money doesn't mean much to the GI. The people were very nice, though, and nobody minded their selling to us at those prices. I bought some pins for Aurelie, Dot and Tess too, but I don't have time to fix them now – more later.'

'One of my buddies had been to Paris,' he continued later that day. 'He bought (out of what I loaned him for the trip) a pair of earrings for you. They are from the Maison le Blanc, or some such name. They are really gaudy things, and big – you said you liked them that way. I've got a brand-new German helmet for Greg or Joe, and also a belt buckle. The rest of the stuff I'll send home when I get a chance. I also got a pair of Russian binoculars.'

'I saw where some fellow sent his wife some German helmets to use as flowerpots,' Johnny wrote the next day. 'We use them for pots too – very handy sometimes. Usually there are no Jerries handy to pull them down over their ears.' He was delighted to have received a Valentine's card from Margaret that day. 'We plan to be in a different country in the next couple of days,' he wrote. 'We are all looking forward to getting back into those German towns again. We don't have anything to do with the civilians there except to tell them to move out. We don't sleep in the barns there. Right now we are in a very nice city. The people here speak mostly German, but they don't have any love for the Nazis. They had the Americans here before the German counter-offensive. There were SS men here when the Germans came in. They did everything to destroy the homes and property of the people. The windows in every building were knocked out. They picked up anybody they wanted and sent them to Germany. We are staying in the home of a doctor. He was taken, but his father and mother are still here. Our kitchen is in a store. I talked to a little girl whose family own the store. Her father was taken about three years ago. They haven't heard from him in over six months. All the people are happy to have us back. They treat us very well. All we need is a bar of chocolate and we get nearly anything. Nothing in the line of food goes to waste. They take our garbage for the hogs and even scrape our cook-pots for food. America is really a lucky nation. We are almost ready now to finish up this war. The chaplain told the boys to put a little more into their prayers. Well, darling, take good care of yourself and Ryle and Thumperess – I'll write as soon as I can. All my love is yours, John.'

The Battle of the Bulge was over and the Allies were victorious. Patton told his men that they were now launching the final offensive and there would be no let-up until Germany surrendered unconditionally. Johnny's letter was postmarked 31 January 1945; later that day he was killed in action near Winterspelt after crossing the Our river into Germany. Five enlisted men from his company were killed on the same day and three others were hospitalised with wounds. Two weeks later, on the eve of St Valentine's Day, Margaret received the dreaded telegram:

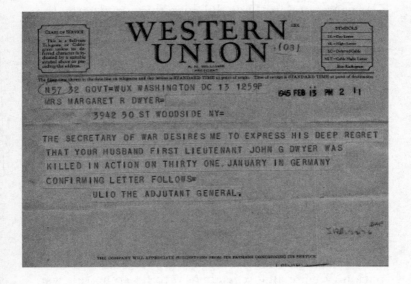

WESTERN UNION

N57 32 GOVT=WUX WASHINGTON DC 13 1259P
MRS MARGARET R DWYER=
    3942 50 ST WOODSIDE NY=

THE SECRETARY OF WAR DESIRES ME TO EXPRESS HIS DEEP REGRET
THAT YOUR HUSBAND FIRST LIEUTENANT JOHN G DWYER WAS
KILLED IN ACTION ON THIRTY ONE JANUARY IN GERMANY
CONFIRMING LETTER FOLLOWS=
    ULIO THE ADJUTANT GENERAL.

9

GOING TO IRELAND AGAIN

Jim Philbin, the detective living downstairs, drove Margaret to the hospital on the day that her second son, Seán, was born: 12 March 1945. Despite her assurance that there was plenty of time, he drove as if he was in a police chase, going through stop signs and running red lights. At one point, a cop on a motorcycle gave chase with his siren blaring, but Jim held out his detective's shield and shouted that it was a medical emergency. The motorcycle cop just waved to him and turned around. 'That bastard's no Irishman,' Jim snapped. 'If he was, he'd escort us to the hospital.' This time Margaret arrived at the hospital without the sirens blazing.

Johnny had taken out two life-insurance policies. One was for $10,000; the other, for $7,000, was initially to cover the student loan he had taken out to attend Lehigh University. The loan was automatically written off by the state following his death, so the insurance money was to be paid in full. He had named Margaret as his sole beneficiary in his will, and he referred to the insurance policies as money that would go to her, but he had never actually altered the terms of the policy to cover the student loan drawn up in the 1930s. When he took out the loan, he had specified that any surplus was to be divided between his father and his aunt Nellie Dwyer, who had been like a mother to him – and was often mistaken for such.

Nellie came up with a fantastic story that one of Johnny's sergeants had come and told her that he was not dead but had been so seriously wounded that he had very little quality of life, and that this news was being withheld from the family. As a result, she said it would be dishonest to cash the insurance cheque. Margaret had the story checked out with the Department of Defence to learn whether there was any truth to it. The whole thing was apparently a figment of Nellie's imagination. It seemed that she had become mentally unhinged following the news of Johnny's death.

Margaret never did learn what happened to any of the money from the policy taken out while he was at university. Over the years, she remained adamant that there should be no mention of the whole thing to the children – which would suggest that she saw it as the ultimate betrayal of her husband. But then she felt that he had been betrayed as a child, and she was more interested in putting that behind her and getting on with her own life. The other policy for $10,000 was paid to her at $55.10 a month over twenty years. By American standards, her war widow's pension and the insurance money, at $148.70 a month, did not amount to much. She had to go back to work.

Ray Bell, a famous horse breeder and racehorse owner who was married to a sister of Johnny's stepmother, used his influence with his friend Howard Hughes to get her a job as a senior reservations clerk for TWA at La Guardia Airport. Of all the companies that Hughes controlled, TWA was the one he most cherished. He fancied himself as an aeroplane designer. He designed the infamous *Spruce Goose*, a wooden plane which never really flew because it was too heavy, but he also played a major part in designing the *Constellation* plane, which went into service in 1946. Although he made his money from other companies, he lavished most of his attention on TWA. He had a major stake in the company, but it was nothing like a controlling share, yet he meddled in its day-to-day affairs and acted as if he was the sole owner. Hughes sometimes called on even the most junior employees to report personally to him. He paid little heed to proper business practices: he often commandeered a TWA plane to fly friends or associates to New York or Hollywood, or even to Europe, leaving the airport staff to facilitate the passengers who had been stranded. As a reservations clerk, Margaret found working for TWA particularly difficult, as it was so badly run, especially in comparison with AT&T.

In view of the interference by Hughes, it was hardly surprising that the company lost what was then a staggering $19 million in the first three years after the war. Margaret initially found the atmosphere at TWA rather strained, as it was known that Hughes had been personally involved in her appointment, and people suspected that she might be reporting directly to him. Of course, this was not the case: she never had any contact with him. In fact, before long he became a recluse and

145

vanished from the public eye altogether.

While working at TWA, Margaret saw the first commercial flight from La Guardia to Rineanna (now Shannon Airport). Ray Bell was on the flight, so Margaret took time off from TWA to see him off, and she was invited to the champagne reception.

Before long, Margaret found it very difficult to combine her work with bringing up two young children. Much of what she earned went on childminders. She quit her job at TWA and began looking after the children full-time. Her mother and Margaret Furlong helped out with the rent. A friend persuaded her to enroll Seán with a child-modelling agency, and he received a number of engagements. He was used on the cover of one popular magazine and also appeared in advertisements in a number of magazines and newspapers, including the *New York Times*. In September 1947, when the Kerry football team came over to New York to play Cavan in the all-Ireland football final, Margaret bought tickets for her mother, Therese and herself for the celebratory dinner, which was held before the game. Mary protested that she would not know anyone there, but she was hardly inside the door when she met John Joe Sheehy, who immediately invited her to the top table. He had been prominent in the IRA and knew that she had helped out his friends back in the 1920s.

While attending Mass at St Patrick's Cathedral in New York City the following St Patrick's Day, Margaret decided to visit Ireland again on a summer holiday, this time with the two boys. The Defence Department was putting pressure on her to decide whether or not she wished to have Johnny's remains repatriated to the United States. He had been buried in a military cemetery in Luxembourg, but now the bodies were being brought back, if the families wished. 'I am an escapist. I run away from situations I can't confront,' she later explained. 'Even when the army asked me whether I wanted John buried in Luxembourg or at home, I couldn't sign the form.' She decided to go to Ireland and think about it.

When Johnny went to Europe first and Margaret's letters were not reaching him, her aunt Gerty Ryle had written to him from Tralee to see if he would get a letter from Ireland. He wrote back from 'Somewhere in Germany', thanking her, the week before Christmas 1944. 'Some day I hope I can take my little family and visit all of you,' he wrote. 'In my very imaginative and lonely hours here, I sometimes think that if I remain here in the army of occupation I'll bring Margaret and Ryle and ? [Ryle's brother Seán, who had not yet been born] over to live in Ireland. Then I'll be able to fly over to see them once in a while.' He had been a keen amateur photographer and had a valuable collection of camera equipment. Margaret had intended to keep these things for the children, but she was advised that the equipment would be obsolete by the time they were old enough to use it, so she sold it; the money paid for a trip to Ireland on the *Mauritania* in May 1948.

They stayed at 3 Greenview Terrace at the home of Margaret's aunt Gerty, who had married Mick McLoughlin in the interim. It proved ideal for Margaret and her sons. Three of her aunts were living in Tralee, and the youngest of their children was only a year older than Ryle. 'We were surrounded by such a big family,' she explained. 'It was great for the boys and great for me. My first impression of Tralee compounded and grew. I loved it.'

'The kids are grand, thank God,' she wrote to Therese, in New York. 'They sure love it here. Really it is amazing how independent they are – and go off by themselves. The only time I ever look for them is at mealtime, and usually they turn up by themselves for it.' There was no way that anyone could leave a four-year-old and a three-year-old to wander off on their own in New York. There was very little traffic then in Tralee, and most of it was horse- or donkey-drawn.

Gerty McLoughlin had a large house with six bedrooms and just herself, her husband, Mick Joe, and his brother Leo, a local rate collector, living there. They could not have been more welcoming. Gerty and Mick Joe had married late and had no children, which was a great pity, because they had a tremendous way with children. He had a wonderful sense of fun, and Gerty had a very good sense of humour, even though she was one of those big, bossy women who wasn't given to minding her own business and was overly concerned about the views of her neighbours. Mick Joe and Leo would play on that. Each year at Christmas, Gerty would regale visitors with the embarrassing exploits of the two brothers. One year the two of them and a lodger next door did not get home until around seven o'clock on Christmas morning, but rather than coming in, they paraded up and down the terrace serenading her, singing 'The Rose of Mooncoin'. 'What do the neighbours think?' Gerty kept saying for days afterwards. Another year Leo came home early on

Christmas Eve. He had obviously had enough to drink already. A messenger boy arrived with mince pies for Gerty. Leo took them from the boy outside the house, 3 Greenview Terrace, but then apparently became disorientated and went to Number 5. He tried to open the front door with his key and could not understand why it would not fit, when the elderly woman of the house suddenly opened the door in her night attire. She had retired early. Leo, realising his mistake, acted quickly. 'Happy Christmas,' he said, handing the bemused woman Gerty's minced pies. Gerty took great delight in explaining why she had no mince pies that Christmas.

In the early war years, Michael Joe and Leo's sister, Violet, had stayed there with her husband, Pat O'Connell, and two children. O'Connell was a garda detective. In 1942, some Kerry people were wanted for the murder of Garda Detective Denny O'Brien in Dublin. Among those wanted was for the killing were two Tralee men: Charlie Kerins, the acting chief of staff of the IRA, and Tadhg Drummond, who was a first cousin of Gerty. In 1944, Pat O'Connell arrested Kerins in Dublin, and he was hanged for the murder later that year. Although the evidence against him was not compelling, the government was determined to make an example of him, convinced that even if he was not the trigger-man, as acting chief of staff of the IRA, he had ordered the murder. The government insisted on hanging him, rather than providing him with a soldier's death before a firing squad. To add further insult to injury, the government brought over the English hangman to do the job.

When the Taoiseach, Éamon de Valera, visited Tralee for the first time in the general election campaign of 1948, he received a rather stormy reception. As he was speaking from a platform in front of the Grand Hotel, Nanette Barrett, a niece of de Valera's old colleague Austin Stack, was shrieking 'Murderer!' at him from one of the upstairs rooms of the Grand Hotel which overlooked the platform. In fact, tension was running so high at the time that the local IRA decided to kill Pat O'Connell in retaliation for the execution of Kerins. Tadhg Drummond tipped off Gerty McLoughlin's brother-in-law Con Kennedy, the town clerk, who was married to Gerty's sister Anne. The IRA plan was to kill O'Connell at his home in Dublin. Drummond's mother probably did not know the story, but she always maintained that Pat O'Connell was a gentleman. Any time he raided her home while Tadhg was on the run, following the murder of Detective Denny O'Brien, O'Connell always insisted that they were looking for a person and the raiding party had no need to break crockery or empty drawers. Now Tadhg Drummond returned the compliment. O'Connell was tipped off to make sure that there was nobody at his home when the IRA called. He sent his family to Tralee and moved into Dublin Castle himself. Armed men did arrive at his home while he was away, so he and his family moved into Dublin Castle permanently, and he lived there for most of the next twenty years.

During the summer of 1948, Margaret decided to remain permanently in Tralee, because she believed it would provide a safe environment in which the children could grow up. Once Margaret decided to stay, she was determined to get a place for the family, but housing was very scarce. For some months she got a large flat in the centre of town, in the Mall over Ryle & Nolan's. Ryle and Sean shared a bedroom in the back, which had a rather unusual view: it overlooked the open toilet in the yard of Toomey's public house. They used to amuse themselves throwing potatoes or coal at the men doing their business below. The patrons of Toomey's might have been prepared for hail, rain or snow from the sky over that toilet, but coal and potatoes must have come as a surprise. Mr Rocket, the manager, who had a flat on the floor above them, must have been a gentle soul, because he never complained. He just arrived up one day with a mixed box of coal and potatoes. He told a bemused Margaret than he was returning them. It was his way of giving a subtle hint that he would rather that the children stop pelting his customers. That ended that little game.

Margaret had her own complaint shortly afterwards when she thought that Mr Rocket's cats spent the whole night fighting. But he told her that he had no cats and that the sound was rats in the walls. The building was constructed on the bank of the river that flowed under the main street and the houses were infested with rats. The vermin delivered their *coup de grâce* during a dinner party one night when a live mouse fell out of the ceiling and landed on the dinner table, causing consternation.

*

Therese came over to Ireland in 1949, allowing Margaret to return to New York in August of that year to close up her flat and move her furniture to Ireland. 'My mother was not happy that I moved here,' Margaret told Breda

151

Joy. 'My father-in-law thought I should be institutional-ised, taking my children from the land of opportunities.' Her living-room and dining-room furniture was very bulky to ship, and she was approached by Mimi Zimmerman to transport a trunk of guns for the IRA. Mimi, who had married a German-American in New York, was a sister of Tadhg Drummond. She acted as if she really believed that Ireland was ready to rise up once the guns had been delivered. Margaret flatly refused. She had no intention of getting involved in Irish politics.

Leaving America was not really that difficult for her, because the political climate there was turning poisonous, with the advent of the McCarthy era. Irish-Americans were becoming distinctly disillusioned as an influx of immigrants flooded the Irish neigbourhoods, and the Irish were beginning their flight to the suburbs. They were also switching their political allegiance to the Republican Party. Mary Harrigan had become disillusioned with Franklin Roosevelt in 1940 and supported the un-successful candidacy of James A. Farley for the Democratic nomination. Four years later, she actively supported the Republican governor of New York, Thomas E. Dewey, for the presidency. She supported him again in 1948 but became disillusioned with Dewey's lacklustre campaign. He was regarded as a certainty to win and ran a bland campaign, trying not to offend anybody. When it came to voting, Mary felt sorry for President Harry Truman, who had barnstormed the county.

That year the Democratic Party was split three ways. Roosevelt's former vice-president, Henry Wallace, was running for the Progressive Party, and the southern

Democrats were supporting Strom Thurmond on a states'-rights ticket. Truman was so far behind in the opinion polls that polling was suspended during the final two weeks of the campaign. Mary felt that the president did not deserve to be badly beaten, so, in the privacy of the polling booth, she voted for Truman, convinced that he was going to lose anyway. Much to her horror, he actually won the election. But she was even more horrified a couple of years later when some Puerto Ricans tried to kill Harry Truman. 'What do you think of the attempt on the life of the president?' she wrote to Margaret. 'Those damn Puerto Ricans, they come over here, fill our hospitals, get all the new apartments in the federal housing, go on relief the day they get here. As a matter of fact, the fellow that was killed by the guards was on relief getting $125 a month. The other fellow was making $75 a week as a brass-polisher in Jersey. They both were our neighbours here in 114th Street. Nice people?'

Margaret was more disillusioned by the rise of right-wing intolerance in the United States as the Republicans targeted the entertainment industry, supposedly in search of Communist infiltrators. Although Margaret never had the least involvement with socialist politics, she knew people who had been involved with socialists and realised that they were sincere idealists. Now, however, people who befriended them frequently became suspects themselves. John Carmody from Tralee, one of the young men that Mary Harrigan had put up in the early 1920s, had become a card-carrying Communist. Shortly before the war, Margaret and her mother had bumped into him at Grand Central Station in New York. He was wearing a

Russian fur hat and proudly carrying a copy of the *Daily Worker*, the Communist newspaper. He had it turned so that the title was in clear view. He said that he had recently returned from the Soviet Union, where things were really great, according to him. 'For God's sake grow up and have some sense,' Mary told him. 'And turn that paper inside out.' She had helped him without regard for his politics, because he was from Tralee. She would undoubtedly have done so again, if he needed help. But people like her were now being identified as a supposed threat to society.

One of those being targeted at the time was Margaret's old seat-mate in grade school, Judy Tuvim – or Judy Holliday, as she was now known. Her grandparents had fled tsarist Russia. Even as a young girl, Margaret knew that Judy had strong liberal and socialist leanings. Thus she became a target of the politicians and right-wing media, especially after she won the Oscar for best actress for her role as Billie Dawn in the movie *Born Yesterday*. She played the part of the blonde bimbo and immortalised the line: 'Do me a favour, Harry – drop dead!' When she rose to speak after being awarded the Oscar, her live radio link was cut. In the light of what subsequently happened, this was possibly more than a coincidence. Judy was pilloried by the Hearst newspaper chain, and some politicians got in on the act because it afforded them easy publicity. She was investigated by the FBI, but it found no evidence that she had ever joined the Communist Party or that she had ever even attended a Communist Party meeting.

She did, however, support a number of causes espoused

by liberals, such as opposing censorship and supporting civil rights. For instance, she supported the campaign of the National Association for the Advancement of Coloured People on behalf of six young black men who had been convicted of murder and sentenced to death in Trenton, New Jersey, even though four of them had alibis to prove that they were elsewhere at the time of the murder. The only witness to the murder had said that the culprits were white. Eventually the cases against all the 'Trenton Six' were overturned on appeal. Yet Judy Holliday had her loyalty and patriotism questioned because she had the integrity and courage to speak out against this obvious miscarriage of justice. Some Communists undoubtedly supported the campaign for the Trenton Six, but that did not mean that all those who supported the campaign were part of a Communist front. 'I am against censorship. I am against persecution of minority races and religions. I am against curtailment of civil liberties,' Judy Holliday declared in a formal statement. "Because of these beliefs, I have on occasion allied myself with others I believed to feel the same way. Some of these groups are now cited as subversive. If that is so, I can only say that I had no knowledge of that allegation at the time of any of my associations with them. My activities were motivated only by idealism and good faith in the aims and principles of such groups as they were represented to me.' These groups included the Independent Citizens Committee of the Arts, Sciences and Professions, the Stop Censorship Committee, Scientific and Cultural Conferences for World Peace, the World Federation of Democratic Youth and the Negro Arts

Committee. She was also questioned about her support for Henry Wallace's presidential campaign in 1948. Wallace had served as Franklin D. Roosevelt's vice-president from 1941 until March 1945, when Harry Truman took over, becoming president less than six weeks later.

When Judy Holliday was called to testify before the US Senate, she made a bit of a farce of the whole thing by playing the part of Billie Dawn, the empty-headed blonde. She dressed as Billie Dawn would have dressed and espoused the same kind of logic, presenting herself as a kind of nitwit. She got the senators feeling sorry for her by saying that she had not realised that the various organisations she had supported were Communist fronts. She admitted that she knew that her uncle Joe Gollomb was a Communist, 'But he broke with the Communist Party around 1941 and has been rabidly anti-Communist ever since,' she said.

When asked if she knew that the writer Thomas Mann was a Communist, she played ignorant. 'How could I know about Mann's record?' she asked.

'And Mr Albert Einstein – do you know the Communist–front record he has?' the committee counsel pressed.

At this point she used the logic that Billie Dawn would have used: 'Then I am sure that Mann and Einstein got into it the way I did, because I am sure none of them are Communists. I mean, if you are a Communist, why go to a Communist front. Why not *be* a Communist? Whatever you are, be it!'

'Well, I guess you've learned to watch it now, haven't

you?' Senator Arthur Watkins of Utah asked.

'Ho, ho! Have I ever!' she replied. 'Now I don't say yes to anything, except cancer, polio and cerebral palsy.'

The senators were laughing at Billie Dawn, but they were the butt of Judy Tuvim's contempt. She had made fools of them, and they deserved it.

10

THE MERRY WIDOW

Although Margaret's pension and insurance payments were meagre by American standards, they translated into £597 for 1949, which was more than twice the average industrial wage in Ireland at the time. By 1951, with the impact of the devaluation of the pound in Ireland, her income jumped to £718, which was almost three times the average industrial wage – then a little over £5 a week. Margaret could even afford a maid. At the time the maid lived in the house and ate with the family. She was paid £1.50 a week, which would have amounted to only $6 a week in the United States. It was pathetic by American standards, but it was more than the going rate in Ireland. One businesswoman complained to Margaret that she was spoiling it for the other employers in town by paying above the odds.

The family was also able to afford to go to Ballybunion on holidays. During their third summer there, she and her cousins the Kennedys rented adjoining houses for a month, but there was an incident that turned Margaret off the beach. A man got into difficulty in the sea; although he was rescued, he subsequently died. Margaret was so upset by the incident that she did not go back to Ballybunion on holidays for another ten years.

While Margaret was acting primarily in the interests of her sons, she did not find Kerry limiting herself. 'We were always going to put our feet up for the winter but we never got round to it,' she recalled. 'And you see, you could afford to have a maid here.' There were so many family members that there was no problem getting a babysitter, with so many relatives in the area.

Among the friends Margaret made in Tralee were Maudie and Tom Ryle, Florence and Sheila O'Connor, Joe and Maeve Grace, Dan Nolan, Ned Nolan, Jo Hussey, Nancy Caball, Norrie and Harry Laide, Donie and Jean Browne, Storeen and Gerty O'Sullivan, Mary and Paddy Hogan, and Barney O'Connor. Therese worked for Traly Footware and was transferred to Dublin to run a showroom for the factory. In the early 1950s there was a fairly close-knit American community in Dublin; it included the future professor of Irish history at the University of Notre Dame, Father Ed Murray, then studying at University College Dublin; historian Jerry Judge and his wife, Eleanor; the singer Pat Thompson; the Libby sisters – Ruth and Elaine; and the actor Carroll O'Connor, who would later turn the character Archie Bunker into a cult figure in the United States. Therese was friendly with them and most of them visited Tralee on breaks.

Father Murray was an extraordinary individual. He had served as an army chaplain in the Second World War and then went back to university to secure a Master's degree from UCD and a doctorate from University College Cork. On one occasion when Margaret Dwyer was with

Father Murray in a hotel lobby in Cork, a large group of people entered the hotel. There was a function to mark a major expansion to the Coca-Cola plant in the city, and James A. Farley, the president of Coca-Cola, was in attendance. As President Roosevelt's campaign manager, Farley was reputed never to forget a face, and he provided evidence of this skill. On entering the hotel lobby, he recognised Father Murray and went over to chat to him, calling him by name. He invited Margaret and Father Murray to join him as his guests at the top table. Afterwards, Father Murray explained that he had met Farley only once, and that was momentarily – in a receiving line when he first graduated from Notre Dame before the war.

In 1951, Margaret rented a house for the family in Castle Countess; she later rented a house in St Brendan's Park and has lived there since 1955. The schools were good in Tralee, though the Christian Brothers primary school had the drawbacks of many Irish schools at the time. There was one particular Christian Brother who molested children not just over years but over decades. Many children who were molested by this Brother would later say that they would not have been believed if they had told their parents about the behaviour of that particular individual. The interference was really in a relatively mild form, involving kissing and touching that fell short of fondling. The individual was in Tralee for some thirty years and the children he molested included the sons of men he had molested as boys. Hence they knew what was going on, but none of them dared to speak out.

The boys knew that Margaret would have confronted

the issue, but this would have entailed the risk of her being depicted as some kind of crazy Yank making scurrilous and unfounded allegations against a religious person. As a result, neither of the boys ever mentioned it at home.

Mary Harrigan, Margaret's mother, retired to Ireland in 1957. She had travelled over each year for a visit by plane, but now she and Margaret Furlong came back for good. Mary travelled by boat this time. Con Kennedy and Michael O'Connor, two of her brothers-in-law, went to Cobh to help with the luggage. Mary was delayed at Customs because she had difficulty locating a trunk that Mimi Zimmerman had asked her to bring home. They knew that Mimi had asked Margaret to bring guns, so they immediately feared the worst, but it turned out that the trunk contained only linen and the like, which Mimi was sending home to her mother and family. Mary Harrigan and Margaret Furlong rented a house together in Castle Countess, which was only a matter of yards from the Christian Brothers secondary school, so Seán and Ryle used to have their dinner there in the middle of the day throughout the school year.

Economically, Tralee was very depressed in the 1950s. The Traly Footware boot factory was reduced to a three-day week, and one of the town's bacon factories was on the brink of closure. The few industries pursued in the town were in trouble. Many men went to work in England, sending home money to support their families, while other families emigrated en masse. Jim Philbin, the New York detective who drove Margaret to hospital on the day that Seán was born, visited Tralee on a number of his trips home to Galway. He told of meeting a waitress in New York. When the waitress told Jim that she was from Tralee, he asked if she knew Margaret Dwyer. She didn't, until he explained that she was a Yank with two sons. 'Oh, yes,' she said. 'We called her the Merry Widow.'

The year 1957 marked the beginning of an upturn. There had been horse racing in Tralee since 1790, and the Irish Racing Board had decided to extend the town's annual two-day race meeting to three days. In an attempt to boost the meeting, the business community decided to establish a simultaneous carnival. There had been a pageant in 1939, during which Eithne O'Sullivan from Valentia Island had been crowned pageant queen, and a further pageant was held the following year, but then the whole thing was abandoned due to the difficulties associated with travel during the war years. In 1957, the concept was revived, with the crowning of Doreen Sheehy as carnival queen. Like the earlier carnival, the new one lasted only two years before giving way to a festival.

The second carnival included an exhibition game of golf between Harry Bradshaw, who had been beaten in a two-way play-off for the British Open title a few years earlier, and Christy O'Connor, who had been in a tie for the lead in the British Open but had just missed out on a play-off by dropping a shot on the final hole. The other two making up the exhibition four-ball were Joe Carr, the British Amateur Open champion, and the amateur international Dr Billy O'Sullivan of Killarney. Just after the exhibition match, Bradshaw and O'Connor headed off for Mexico City, where they won the prestigious Canada (now World) Cup of Golf.

While discussing the success of the second carnival, some local businessmen came up with the idea of developing on the carnival-queen concept. The businessmen – Dan Nolan, publisher of the *Kerryman*; his half-brother Ned (Aggie) Nolan; Florence O'Connor, a local butcher; Joe Grace, a solicitor and secretary of the local race company; and Roger Harty, in whose pub they held the discussion – came up with the idea of exploiting 'The Rose of Tralee', a very popular nineteenth-century love song written by a Tralee merchant, William Pembroke Mulchinock, about Mary O'Connor, a local servant girl with whom he fell in love and who died while he was away in India.

They decided to invite people in Britain and the United States to send contestants to select a 'Rose of Tralee'. Dan Nolan went to New York, where Mike Reidy, a Kenmare expatriate, suggested that they use the name 'The Festival of Kerry' as a more all-embracing title. Because of her American background, Margaret Dwyer was invited to join the new organizing committee. There were many facets to the committee, as the enterprise incorporated myriad events. This required an enormous amount of voluntary input, in both organising and stewarding the events.

The organisers of the Festival of Kerry were lucky in that it first took place in 1959, when Ireland was on the verge of major changes. Éamon de Valera had finally stepped down from active politics and was replaced by Seán Lemass, who set about building on the economic miracle of T. K. Whitaker's National Development Plan. The government had finally recognised the importance of tourism.

Of course, tourism had always been important to

Killarney, which had been probably the premier tourist destination in Ireland since Queen Victoria visited the area to see the lakes in 1861. But many Kerry people were turned off both by the fawning attitude that many people adopted towards foreigners in Killarney and by their mercenary behaviour, such as charging for tap water on a particularly hot day Munster football final Sunday. Whenever Margaret was in Killarney and she, or visiting American friends, wished to purchase anything, Seán or Ryle would be told to ask the price, because they had Kerry accents. If Margaret said something with her New York accent, the price would go up immediately. This kind of thing gave tourism a bad name and undoubtedly retarded its development in the county.

The Festival of Kerry, which was primarily designed to put Tralee on the tourist map, was in an ideal position to exploit the new focus on tourism. The festival was able to capitalise on well-placed Kerry people in the civil service in Dublin, as well as Kerry emigrants who had been successful abroad. These people were now eager to do something for their native county. The Festival of Kerry provided an outlet for men like Brian K. Sheehy, a transport inspector in New York; Billy Clifford in London; and John Byrne, who had recently returned to Dublin after making his fortune in construction and dance halls in Britain.

The plan for the initial festival was for five girls to be selected as contestants from New York, London, Birmingham, Dublin and Tralee. Dan Nolan went to the United States to line up people to handle the New York end of things. The committee had a huge two-and-a-half-ton lighted emblem of a red rose with green leaves, and 'The Festival of Kerry' spelt out in white lights beneath. The sign was lit by some four hundred lights. The emblem, which cost more than £200 out of the committee's £750 budget for the year, was hung on the front of the Ashe Memorial Hall.

About a hundred and fifty people travelled from New York for the festival in the last week of August 1959. The first part of the group from New York arrived in Shannon on Saturday, greeted by a convoy of some eighty cars from Tralee. The country's tourism industry was still very poorly organised at the time and it was significant that the first charter for the Festival of Kerry from New York was run by a Dutch airline, KLM. The mayor of Limerick was at the airport to meet the group, along with the chairman of Ennis Urban District Council. The visitors were treated to an Irish-coffee reception and each was presented with an official-looking Kerry passport, which was then stamped at the Feale Bridge by a uniformed Customs officer as the cavalcade of cars entered Kerry. The State Solicitor, Donal Browne, supplied the mock passports. When the cavalcade reached the outskirts of Tralee, the cars were led through the streets of the town to the Ashe Memorial Hall by mounted horsemen, torch-bearers, and four bands. Two of these – St Joseph's Boys' Brass Band and Gill Brien's Band – were local, and they were joined by the Laune Pipers' Band, and the Millstreet Pipe Band. About twenty thousand people lined the streets.

A second aeroplane carrying some seventy-five people had to return to Gander, Newfoundland, due to engine trouble, and it did not arrive in Shannon until the following day. Many of the passengers were coming specially for the unveiling of the new monument in Ballyseedy to commemorate IRA people killed during the War of Independence and the Civil War. The monument itself was near the site where eight IRA men had been massacred in March 1923 during the Civil War. Nine IRA prisoners had been taken by soldiers of the Free State government from the jail in Tralee and driven to Bally-seedy, where they were tied around a mine, which was then detonated. By some freak, in the explosion one of the men, Stephen Fuller, was blown clear, and he managed to escape to tell the tale. It was the worst atrocity of the Civil War. Although this had nothing to do with the Festival of Kerry, John Joe Sheehy, the head of the organising committee for the monument, was the father of Kathleen Sheehy, the young woman chosen to repre-sent Tralee in the Rose contest.

Members of the festival committee represented the whole spectrum of political opinion but they managed to keep the festival nonpolitical. Billy Clifford, who had organised the London selection, had fought in the Civil War on the Free State side. Most of the young men from Tralee who had taken part in the war were on the republican side; Clifford was one of the six young Tralee men who had joined the Free State army and who became known as 'the Dandy Six'. On returning for the festival, he found himself sharing the back seat of a car with one of his republican contemporaries, to whom he had not spoken since the Civil War. By the time they reached Tralee, they had shaken hands and were chatting affably, having decided to bury the past. Political feelings were still running very high in some quarters, however. For instance, Stephen Fuller, the lone survivor of the Ballyseedy massacre, was not invited to the unveiling of the monument, because he had joined Fianna Fáil in the 1930s.

On the night of the unveiling of the Ballyseedy monument, there was a big festival banquet at the CYMS Hall in Tralee. The Great Southern Hotel, Killarney, did the catering and some three hundred people attended. The next night there was a festival dance in the hall, where the selection of Alice O'Sullivan of Dublin as the Rose of Tralee was witnessed on closed-circuit television from the Ashe Memorial Hall. This in itself was a novel event for the people of Tralee, as the advent of television proper in the area was still a few years off. Through his media contacts, Dan Nolan had assembled a distinguished battery of media people in the Ashe Memorial Hall. They included camera crews from the BBC, Twentieth-Century Fox and International Newsfilms Ltd. 'The whole proceedings will be on television shortly,' Vincent Corcoran, the BBC cameraman, told the *Kerryman*. 'In addition, sixteen copies of our film will be sent abroad. Over 100 million TV viewers will see it abroad.'

The judges of the Rose of Tralee contest were Michael Mulchinock, a great-grand-nephew of the man who wrote 'The Rose of Tralee'; Walter Smithwick, director of Smithwicks Brewery, Kilkenny; Frank Bandy of Rank Films of London; *Evening Press* columnist Terry O'Sullivan; and Lord Harrington, who was chosen because of his involvement in horse racing. Margaret Dwyer was given the job of asking Harrington to be a judge in the contest. He liked the idea, and his only question was whether he should bring his own measuring tape. Margaret explained that there would be no swimsuit element to the contest. The judges would have to look for the elusive quality suggested by the words of the song: 'It was not her beauty alone that won me.'

Myriad open competitions were arranged, including a donkey derby, a tug-of-war competition, and 'tossing the sheaf' in the town park; a terrier derby in Rock Street; a bicycle race around the houses; and both a swimming race and a kayak race in the canal. There was also a handball competition in the Fitzgerald-Jones Alley (now the site of the folk theatre Siamsa Tíre). In addition, there was a children's race and a fancy-dress parade for children. There were also three days of horse racing. During the festival, betting on the tote at the racecourse was up by more than 20 per cent on the previous year.

The great novelty items of that festival were a fireworks display and a sheepdog-trials demonstration by John Evans from Wales. Most people had never seen sheepdog trials. Evans brought over six dogs for a demonstration in the town park. Some eighty thousand people thronged into the town that night; this had an enormous impact on a town with a population of around ten thousand. Arrangements had been made for Evans to stay at a local hotel, where an outhouse had been prepared for his dogs, but he insisted on sleeping with the animals. When the golf club was approached to put up the dogs, it was assumed that they would sleep in the stables out back, but the owner insisted on keeping them in the clubhouse itself.

They were therefore put up together in the ladies' lounge, which had recently been decorated with a new carpet. While the dogs were highly trained in the art of driving sheep, they were not house-trained, and the resulting mess in the ladies' lounge did little for tempers on all sides.

Margaret's main task on the festival committee was to look after the entertainment of sponsors, visiting dignitaries and their wives. The guests included the US ambassador, Scott McLoud. One of the functions at the festival was a 'Winkler Club', a party featuring shellfish. John Byrne, who had recently returned to Ireland with plans to build O'Connell Bridge House in Dublin, was a native of Kilflynn, County Kerry. He was honoured by being invested as the 'Grand Winkler', with a chain of office made of seashells. This party was a great success, but it went badly wrong when the organisers tried to repeat it the following year. A horde of gatecrashers descended on the place. When they could not get in the doors, they climbed through windows, including the kitchen window in the steward's residence, where they tore curtains, broke a mop and stole some petty cash. The bar was chaotic. 'Boy! Boy!' one individual kept calling the steward, Tom Roche, a retired army veteran, who studiously ignored him until he could take no more. Then he went to the man and told him in no uncertain terms that there were no boys behind the bar and that he would not be served, even if he shouted for the rest of the night.

Roche's wife put in a claim for £3 17s 6d as a result of the losses and damage caused to family property. The committee agreed to pay it immediately, but at the same time it decided to give Tom Roche two months' notice to quit the premises, as he was being dismissed. One committee member noted that Tom's 'attitude to some members in the bar was almost intolerable'. Roche asked for the reasons for his dismissal in writing, but the committee did not bother to respond. Jack Courtney, the managing director of Traly Footwear and a member of the Festival Committee, appreciated Roche's dedication and honesty, however, and promptly hired him as a security man.

As it was not a tourist town, Tralee did not have the commercial facilities to put up the influx of people who arrived for the festival, but the Festival Committee set up an accommodation bureau to enable people to take in paying guests for bed and breakfast. This was run out of Caball's shop in Bridge Street.

In the second year of the festival, the number of Roses was expanded to nine with the addition of representatives from Boston, Chicago, Leeds and County Kerry. A series of Rose Selection heats were held throughout the winter months, culminating in the selection of a young woman to represent the county. The overall winner in 1960 was the Chicago representative. The judges that year were Sean Keating of New York; Toddy O'Sullivan, the managing director of the Gresham Hotel, Dublin; Commander George Crosbie of the *Cork Examiner*; racehorse owner Rex Beaumont; and Walter Smithwick of the brewery of the same name. One of the features of that festival was the introduction of new-style lights that had been purchased in Blackpool, go-cart racing on a track near the town park, clay-pigeon shooting and a hunting-dog exhibition.

After the fiasco of the second Winkler party at the

golf club, it was decided to entertain the sponsors and guests at a Festival Club in 1961. Barney O'Connor, a former publican and a member of the festival committee, organised a bar in the Forester's Hall in Staughton's Row. The place was specially decorated for the occasion. Various drinks companies were approached for products and they supplied cases of liquor and barrels of stout and beer. The drink was allocated for each night so that it would last throughout the festival. All the drink was free in the Festival Club. The brandy would run out first, then the spirits, and finally the beer and stout. People's choice of the free drink was obviously determined by how much it would normally cost. The Festival Club – which did not open until around 1 AM, when the bars around town officially shut – was a great success. The novelty items that year included a national pipe band competition and motorcycle grass track racing in the town park.

Bertram Mills Circus, which claimed to be the largest circus in Europe, came to Tralee during the 1961 festival. In a strict sense, it was not part of the festival, because the circus charged for admission, but it blended in with the festivities by supplying animals and acts such as clowns, jugglers and stilt-walkers to participate in a parade through the town each morning, along with the various bands. Having elephants and a caged bear, tiger or lion parading through the town added greatly to the festivities.

Margaret Dwyer and Sheila O'Connor were detailed to look after the judges' wives on the night of selection. The only change in the judging panel was the inclusion of Hector Legge, the editor of the *Sunday Independent,* in place of Seán Keating. After the selection, they brought the wives upstairs in the Ashe Memorial Hall to the council chamber, but when they opened the door they found that Terry O'Sullivan and some of the media had their own little game going. Terry was playing the role of doctor, operating on a lady friend who was on a desk, partially covered by a tablecloth and naked from the waist up. But Margaret trod on Commander Crosbie's wife's foot as she tried to back out of the room. Later, when O'Sullivan tried to talk to the Commander's wife, he got a very frosty reception.

The following year, Fossett's Circus was set up in the town park in an open-air format. There was no charge for admission. The Festival organisers paid the circus a fee to put on a show each evening. This suited the circus people, because they did not have the hassle of moving every day. Although they were particularly fortunate with the weather that year, the open-air format proved particularly difficult for the tightrope-walking and trapeze people, because of the evening dew.

Ciara O'Sullivan of Dublin was chosen as Rose of Tralee that year. She later married John Byrne, the builder and property developer. Shortly afterwards, he was instrumental in the building of the Mount Brandon Hotel, which greatly facilitated one of the main goals of the Festival of Kerry – putting Tralee on the tourist map. In 1963, the Festival of Kerry included a major vintage-car rally; the vintage cars were used in the opening parade to ferry the various Roses. The more than thirty cars involved included a 1901 De Dion, a 1914 Rolls Royce, a 1914 Ford Model T, a 1923 Chevrolet and a 1929 Studebaker. The main money-spinner for the festival committee was the nightly dances at the Ashe Memorial Hall, but in 1963 the committee ran into some local competition when the CYMS tried to compete with the festival dances by hiring the internationally famous Acker Bilk and his band. The festival dances at the Ashe Memorial Hall were still filled to capacity; the young group Dickie Rock and the Miami Showband was a tremendous hit. That year the Festival Club moved to the much more spacious Theatre Royal, but it moved back to the Forester's Hall again for the next two years. The overall cost of the festival, covering the wages of three barmen, a steward, caretaker, rent of the hall and chairs, along with the decorating of the hall and all the drink that was given out free, came to less than £200.

Margaret Dwyer was involved in each of the festivals during those years. Her sister, Therese Hassett, emigrated to Canada with her husband, Dr Noel Hassett, and their five children in 1961. They had five more children there.

Seán Dwyer went to university in North Dakota in 1962, and Ryle went to Texas, at the other end of the country. They had grants from the Veterans Administration as a result of their father's death. Both earned doctorate degrees – Seán in chemistry from the University of North Dakota and Ryle in modern European history from the University of North Texas. Margaret frequently spent part of the winter helping out Therese with her ten children in Canada, but she was usually back in Tralee early enough to help represent the Tralee committee at the various preliminary Rose dances held throughout Kerry, and the county final, in which the County Kerry Rose was chosen.

Florence O'Connor, who held shares in Ballybeggan Park, persuaded fellow shareholders to open up the centre of the racecourse free to patrons in order that an aspect of the race meeting would be part of what it was billing as 'the Greatest Free Show on Earth'. Entry to the centre of the course had always been much cheaper, and there were various carnival rides for children in the area, as well as the bookmakers. The race committee noted that they were effectively foregoing the £800 that would normally be taken at the gate. Bord Fáilte and Guinness came on board as major sponsors of the festival in 1965. In order to fill the void, the festival committee arranged a two-day horse-trotting race meeting in the town park. There was also a gymkhana, in which some of the country's top horses competed. The main event was won by the distinguished international rider Tommy Wade, on his famous horse Dundrum. The festivities included an aerial display involving planes, gliders, and helicopters, and a parachute demonstration; Fossett's Circus put on a matinée on the weekday afternoons.

The festival also exploited the growing popularity of folk music by billing itself as 'the Folk Festival of Ireland', as well as 'the Greatest Free Show on Earth'. Some of the horse-drawn tourist carriages were hired, and a folk village was formed in the town park for folk musicians who wished to take part in various music contests. They were provided with the caravans free of charge for the week. Heimatzunft Hufingen, a major German folk group from the Black Forest, were special guests in their traditional costumes, courtesy of the Bonn government, and the German ambassador, Dr Heinz Truetzschler von Falkenstein, attended the festival.

In 1964, a 'Singing Pubs Competition' had been introduced as part of the myriad competitions that were held during the festival. The initial award went to the Wolfe Tones, a relatively unknown group from Dublin who were playing in the Tavern in Boherbee. The competition proved so successful that it was decided to hold three additional musical competitions the following year. They were for the best cabaret act, the best street entertainment (essentially a busking competition) and the Guinness International Folk Award for the best folk group. This last competition was staged in public and was won by Teddy Furey and his three sons, who later became internationally famous as the Furey Brothers. Finbar Furey gave a virtuoso performance on the uilleann pipes that year.

It was generally agreed that the 1965 Festival was the most successful yet. The selection of the Rose of Tralee was televised live for the first time that year. The contest was held in the open air on a stage constructed on the front steps of the Ashe Memorial Hall. Kevin Hilton again hosted the show, and Therese Gillespie of Belfast was chosen as the Rose of Tralee. She later married Tim Collins, a local hotel owner, and settled in the town. The Festival of Kerry and Tralee races ran on different dates in 1966, but this did not seem to affect the success of either event. The race committee had agreed to later dates with the racing board and had not informed the Festival of Kerry. Ironically, once entry to the centre of the racecourse had been made free, it soon killed the popularity of the area. People preferred to pay to get into the normal enclosure. Fossett's Circus had also become a feature of the festivities but it had to introduce a nominal charge, because too many of the same children were taking up seats at every show and others could not get in. The Festival Club was moved to the Ashe Memorial Hall following the construction of the Mount Brandon Hotel in 1966, but organisers found that the crowding at the door became so dangerous that it was decided to sell tickets; things then became so hectic within the hall that they had to charge for alcohol.

Many people used to come down from Belfast for the festival, and they were surprised to find that the unionist anthem, 'The Sash', was particularly popular in the South. Invariably, there would be sing-songs in the pubs and hotels, and somebody would sing 'The Sash'; the Northern visitors would eventually join in and would inevitably remark that nobody was going to believe it when they got home. In 1963, a young Donncha Ó Dúlaing visited the Festival of Kerry to record *Munster Journal* for Radio Éireann. While there, he met the Wolfe Tones for the first time. 'They will sing "The Sash" for you,' somebody said. 'I didn't bat an eyelid, and there and then the Wolfe Tones made what was for them their first radio broadcast,' Ó Dúlaing noted. 'That broadcast was also the first occasion on which any radio critic ever noticed me. One critic wrote in a national daily that he had enjoyed a *Munster Journal* at the Festival of Kerry and had found it extraordinary to hear a group of young men with rather pronounced Dublin accents singing "The Sash" in the deep south!' Of course, this was before the eruption of the troubles in the North, and there was little understanding in Kerry of the sectarian problems north of the border. Some years later, when RTÉ broadcast the song again, a bomb went off near the RTÉ studios in Donny-brook, Dublin; it was felt that the attack was in reaction to the playing of this sectarian song.

In 1967, eligibility for the Rose contest was extended to young women of Irish ancestry, rather than being confined to the granddaughters of Kerry people. The festival itself was beginning to get stale. 'The organisation was founded to put life into Tralee during the week of Tralee Races – more specifically into the pubs and the streets of the town,' festival president Florry O'Connor noted. 'Our objective was simply defined and created no great problems in its first years. The problems arose when our ideas and imagination began to break out of this simple directive. We discovered that dedication and hard work could make what seemed to be impossible reasonable and within our power. During these early years, there was no shortage of ideas or people to implement them. Inevitably, however, as time went by, the strain began to tell. The first festivals were fired by the enthusiasm of a committee determined to prove that it could create a super festival. All the members of the committee were prepared to put their time – and very often their money – on the line to do this. Having more or less achieved this purpose, we on the committee relaxed. The old crusading spirit seem to tire and the momentum of the festival slackened.'

A new lease of life was injected into the festival committee with the decision to introduce floral floats. These were initially decorated with real flowers. 'There was no precedent for what was proposed in this country, and this was exactly the challenge that appealed to the Festival of Kerry committee,' Florry explained. 'The

177

designing, building and decorating of them brought back the old enthusiasm to the festival activity and proved there was life in the old dog yet.' The floats were made by festival members and the staff of a couple of the local factories, Traly Footwear and Kerry Precision Ball. As they were making them, however, the workers insisted on the installation of a television set to view the final episode of *The Fugitive*, a very popular drama series during the 1960s. One of the features at the Festival dances was the appearance of 'the singing priest', Father Michael Cleary.

Seán Dwyer came home for the Festival in 1967 and enrolled as an escort. It was suggested that he should escort Geraldine Healy, the Limerick Rose and the daughter of Margaret's friend Eithne (O'Sullivan) Healy, who had been the first Carnival Queen back in 1939. Seán insisted that he did not want anything to do with the daughters of his mother's friends, but on meeting Geraldine, he promptly changed his mind. It was obviously love at first sight. Before the end of the week, they became informally engaged – he gave her his Delta Upsilon fraternity pin – and they made it formal when he came home again for Christmas 1967. They were married the following August and were back from their honeymoon in time for the next festival.

One of the more memorable aspects of the 1968 festival was the introduction of Terry Wogan as the new host of the Rose Selection. Born in Limerick, he had joined RTÉ in the early 1960s. He did the show again for the next two years. By then, he was already establishing himself in Britain with a daily two-hour radio programme on the BBC. In 1969, one of the judges was Countess Lilly MacCormack, the widow of tenor John McCormack, who helped make the song 'The Rose of Tralee' so famous. The number of places represented in the contest was extended to twenty-three, with Roses drawn from six other countries – Australia, Britain, Canada, France, New Zealand and the USA. Members of the cast of the movie *Ryan's Daughter* were conspicuously present at the festival that year, as the movie was being filmed on location in Kerry at the time. The folk theatre Siamsa Tíre was highlighted on the opening night. One of the features of that year's festival was the employment of a general secretary to run the festival, but in the midst of the changeover a large debt was incurred, and it was necessary to cut back on some of the events in the 1970s.

The Festival of Kerry undoubtedly did more for the image of Tralee during the third quarter of the twentieth century than any other event. It put the town on the map as a visitor destination, and this had a spin-off effect on the whole area. The success of the festival was apparent when the Irish Racing Board allocated the Tralee festival meeting an extra day, bringing it to four days, in 1970. Although the festival normally avoided politics, Brian Lenihan, the Fianna Fáil minister, was invited to open the festivities in 1970 in the midst of a good deal of political intrigue. Earlier in the year, two ministers, Charles Haughey and Neil Blaney, had been arrested on charges of attempted gun-running. Haughey and three other were still awaiting trial during the festival, but he came down to the race meeting along with his father-in-law, the retired Taoiseach Seán Lemass. The Minister for Justice, Des O'Malley, was also present, though he managed to avoid the photographers; both Lenihan and

O'Malley met Haughey in Tralee – much to the chagrin of the Secretary of the Department of Justice, who had Haughey under surveillance. These events were to have repercussions for many years to come.

Florence O'Connor, who had effectively run the festival after taking over from Dan Nolan in 1960, decided to step down after the 1970 event. He had stepped down before and the committee had elected chairmen, and even joint chairmen, but inevitably they would turn to Florence as the festival approached, and he would have to take up the reins again. The only way that he was going to break away was to sever all connections with the Festival of Kerry, but he had no chosen successor. He advised Margaret Dwyer not to consider the position, as he said it was not a job for a woman. 'Women are too bitchy,' he said. None of the capable businessmen would take on the role, however, so Margaret was elected the first woman president of the Festival of Kerry in October 1970. She also had the role of sole chairman. Shortly after she took over, the general secretary notified her that he was resigning, and she quickly had him replaced with the young Ted Keane. 'It's a big challenge for anyone and a bigger challenge for me, because I am a woman,' she told the *Kerryman*.

11

Rose of Tralee

In the early 1970s the whole tourism sector suffered as a result of the Northern troubles, which grew immeasurably worse in 1971. The country was in transition, as was the Festival of Kerry. The generation that had founded the Festival was growing tired. For some, the Festival had achieved its aim, but Margaret Dwyer felt that it was needed more than ever – which made the challenge all the greater.

Margaret Dwyer went to Canada for Christmas 1970. While there, she attended the ceremony at the University of North Dakota at which her son Seán was conferred with a doctorate in chemistry. In January 1971 she set off on a tour of eighteen North American cities, with the aim of persuading Americans and Canadians to come to Kerry for the Festival.

As a New Yorker promoting an Irish festival, she got ready access to the media in both Canada and the United States. She had media interviews in Calgary, Alberta; Great Falls, Montana; Winnipeg, Manitoba; Chicago; South Bend, Indiana; Cleveland, Ohio; Toronto; Philadelphia; New York; and Boston.

In Calgary, where the *Albertan* published her interview with David May, Margaret met some twenty Irish doctors and their wives, along with Irish people working for the local airlines. She persuaded them to establish a committee to select a Rose for that year's Festival. In Great Falls, Margaret met a group of Irish priests who thought they would have no difficulty in establishing a Rose Committee, but she thought they were overly optimistic. In Chicago, Jack Hagerty of WOPA and Wally Phillips of WGN interviewed her.

At the University of Notre Dame, her friend Father Ed Murray, a professor of Irish history, asked her to address his history students, and she was interviewed on WSBT in South Bend and on WJOB in Hammond, Indiana. Brian Murray of CBC TV also interviewed her on *Toronto Today*, and further interviews were published with three daily newspapers in New York City, including the *New York Daily News*, which had the largest circulation of any newspaper in the United States.

A new committee was set up in Lawrence, Massachusetts, and it made arrangements to send a Rose to that year's Festival. Margaret also had discussions with travel agents about the possibility of setting up Rose Committees in Missouri and in Spokane, Washington.

Upon her return to Ireland, she set out on a round of the various Rose dances: she was in London one night, Birmingham the following night, and Brosna, County Kerry, the night after that. During May, she attended the dances in Rathmore, Kenmare and Dingle; she went to the dance in Abbeyfeale in early June and then, later that month, to Killarney for the final to select the Kerry

Rose. In addition, there was at least one executive committee meeting each week. It was a full-time job, and she was able to devote her full attention to it.

In 1970 the town was badly flooded. A river flowed beneath the main street and the arches were damaged in the flood, with the result that it became necessary to stop traffic on a large part of the main street. It seemed that Tralee was crumbling.

During the summer, there were indications that there would be more visitors from abroad, but then the political situation deteriorated dramatically after the British government introduced internment without trial in Northern Ireland in early August. Many people who had planned to travel to the Festival promptly cancelled their arrangements amid the explosion of violence in the North.

'Had the Northern situation not been so bad, we would have had more Americans,' Margaret Dwyer contended. 'Those with no Irish connections and no knowledge of the country look at a map, see what a tiny island we are, and naturally enough, I suppose, imagine that the bullets are flying all over the country.'

In view of the difficulty of attracting foreign visitors, plans were already afoot to make an extra effort to promote the Festival in Ireland. For the first time ever, it was decided that the overseas Roses would fly into Dublin instead of Shannon, in an attempt to exploit coverage in the national media. The plans were announced at a press conference in Dublin in early August. As usual, Terry O'Sullivan waxed lyrical about the Festival in the *Evening Press*. 'In all the years I have known it, the Festival of Kerry has had only one incident that had to have the attention of the law, and that had to do with the finding of a stolen watch in somebody's shoe,' he wrote. 'The holidaymakers and those who will be at work as usual the next morning don't get sick, don't use foul language, don't beat each other, don't break bottles on the pavement or in the gutter, and whole families stay out till the small hours under the brilliant lights. The children store away glamorous memories to be taken out and polished when they are grown-ups.'

As a further promotional gimmick, it was decided that Margaret should fly to Dublin from the new airport in Farranfore in a small Cessna plane owned by 'Kerry Airways' and renamed *The Rose of Tralee* for the occasion. The arrival of the Roses in Dublin was covered by all the national daily newspapers. It was also given plenty of space in the two Dublin evening papers, with Terry O'Sullivan of the *Evening Press* and Tom Hennigan of the *Evening Herald* providing extensive coverage of the event in their social columns.

The foreign contestants were given a chance to see more of the country. Rooms were provided in Dublin, courtesy of the Gresham Hotel, and the Roses travelled to Tralee by special bus, with planned stops at Portlaoise, Nenagh and Limerick. There was also another unplanned stop just outside Dublin, where the Garda Síochána flagged down the bus. Everyone was asked to get out for a photograph, but the real reason for this request was so that the bus could be searched, as a bomb warning had been received. This turned out to be a hoax. At Patrick's Well, a traditional motorcade was laid on, with scheduled stops in Abbeyfeale and Castleisland.

Margaret was supposed to fly back to Farranfore on the same small plane that had brought her to Dublin, but Kerry Airport was fogbound. They had a hair-raising experience as an air-traffic controller talked the pilot down in Shannon: at one point, a transatlantic plane had to be diverted after the air-traffic controller announced that he had lost the small plane on the radar.

The number of Roses that year – twenty-six – was the highest yet. As well as Calgary and Lawrence in North America, there were also two new British centres: Newcastle and Thames Valley. There was supposed to be another Rose from Bristol, where the Four Provinces Club had run an Irish Week at which a Bristol Rose was chosen, but this led to some embarrassment. The women chosen changed jobs shortly afterwards and the club had difficulty contacting her with her travel details. She eventually made it to Tralee, but the Festival had already begun, so the judges decided not to consider her – sparking a brief controversy in the media.

The entertainment for the Festival included the Jack Cruise and Jack O'Connor variety shows appearing each night on one of the two stages on the streets. There were the usual daily parades, which included a number of bands, such as the Army Band of the Southern Command, the New York Police Department Band and Irish marching bands from Limerick, Ballybunion and Millstreet, as well as the local St John's Pipe Band from Tralee. In addition, there were various folk groups, such Volkstanzkreis Passau from Bavaria in Germany, the Killingworth Sword Dancers from England, a Belgian folk group, two Canadian folk groups and a university folk group from

Newcastle-on-Tyne, as well as the Hession dancers from Galway, and a group from the local Siamsa Tíre. Up to 100,000 people were attracted to the town each night.

Going into pubs in Tralee was like trying to shoulder one's way out through a crowd after a Croke Park final, according to Terry O'Sullivan of the *Evening Press*. 'That was the pattern all over this town of Tralee,' he wrote. 'Every pub was a club, every place was full, full of the sound of Kerry talk, full of the smell of fried onions and hot fat from the mobile canteen, that drifted in so smugly under the street lights.

'Here at this moment at the Festival of Kerry, as light-hearted and as innocent as its founder members intended it to be, it is difficult to come to grips with reality,' O'Sullivan continued. 'There is always here the suggestion of being involved in a beautify illustrated fairly tale.'

Attending the Festival of Kerry 'was a bewildering experience, requiring the constitution of an ox,' according to Seamus Kelly of 'Quidnunc' fame in the *Irish Times*. 'All over Tralee there are temporary street theatres where the people can come and look at German folk dancers, the Hession Troupe from Galway, or the Killingsworth Sword Dancers, or the Newcastle Kingsmen, or Punch and Judy shows, or ventriloquists, or any of the umpteen variety shows, all free. If that palls, there is the City of London Girl Pipers, the New York Police Department Pipe Band, Fossett's Famous Circus and a funfair featuring a big dipper called, grandly, "La Souris".'

'As a visitor to the Festival for the first time,' Gus Smith of the *Sunday Independent* wrote, 'I was deeply impressed by the "free show" aspect of it. Well-organised and enjoyable variety and theatre shows were presented on improvised stages in the streets and the shows were immensely enjoyed by thousands.'

Brendan O'Reilly of RTÉ hosted the Rose Selection that year. Linda McCravy from Miami was selected as the Rose of Tralee; she was to do a certain amount of promotional tourism work during the ensuing year.

The Festival came to a rather premature end in 1971. It had been planned to close with a forty-five-minute fireworks display, but this had to be called off because of heavy rain that night. As a neighbourly gesture, the Festival Committee gave the £34,000-worth of fireworks to Listowel for their harvest festival later that month. Some children were injured, however, when they found part of a firework that had not gone off completely at the harvest festival. The Listowel committee washed their hands of any responsibility for the fireworks, and the Festival of Kerry was successfully sued; this added to the company's growing insurance costs.

During November, the author Alice Curtayne slated the Festival of Kerry in an article in the *Sunday Independent* after a visit to the town. Born in Tralee in 1901, she had been educated in England and had established herself as a scholarly author. Among her books were biographies of St Catherine of Siena and Patrick Sarsfield and a book on the poetry of Francis Ledwidge. Her scholarly reputation was not enhanced by her article blaming the Festival of Kerry for the pedestrianisation of part of the centre of Tralee. This had been a safety precaution: the flooding had damaged the arches over which the streets were built. The local Chamber of

Commerce had tried to make a virtue of necessity by making the area as attractive as possible, with seats, flower tubs, umbrellas and a portable fountain. Margaret Dwyer had been asked to open the whole thing officially, but that was the only connection between the new development and the Festival. During the good summer, this area added a kind of Continental flair to the town. Later, when the damage had been repaired, there were public calls, supported by most of the businesses in the area, to retain the pedestrian way, but other parts of the town objected that it would give that part of town an unfair business advantage. In the meantime, there was considerable indignation over Curtayne's article.

'Following a three-year absence, I went back there in recent weeks and saw what had been done to the Mall for the Festival of Kerry,' Curtayne wrote. 'Twelve garden seats, the stock-in-trade of any hardware shop, were set down one half of the way, separated from the other half by a concrete strip.' She blamed the Festival Committee for 'the rape of the Mall.'

'This Festival is a justifiable tourist gimmick,' she added. 'What light does it throw on our distinctive identity here? Does it contain an echo of our austere and proud history? Is everything to be suffered in the name of a tourist gimmick? When will people understand how offensive it is to underestimate in this way the intelligence, education and good taste of our visitors?'

'That a lady of her reputation for scholarship should have so lamentably departed from fact when she came to write for the *Sunday Independent* about her native town made one realise that she had been out of it for so long

that she had lost all contact with it and its problems,'
complained Dan Nolan, the former publisher of the
Kerryman. 'Any local school boy or girl could have told
her, had she taken the trouble to inquire, as any journalist,
free lunch or otherwise, should, that the pedestrianisation
of Upper Bridge Street and one side of the Mall was a
safety measure taken by the public authority owing to
the danger of the town arch collapsing under vehicular
traffic. The Festival of Kerry promoters had as little to do
with the pedestrianisation of Upper Bridge Street and
one side of the Mall as they had to do with the pedestrianisation of Henry Street and Grafton Street in Dublin.

'Nor had the Festival of Kerry promoters anything to
do with the provision of the fountain, the seating, shrubs,
etc, in Upper Bridge Street and the Mall,' Nolan continued. 'These amenities, despite Alice Curtayne's dislike
of them, were provided by the traders at their own expense
to attract shoppers on foot, and nobody can say that they
were not enjoyed by the public during an unusually warm
and dry summer and autumn.'

Margaret Dwyer was re-elected president of the Festival
of Kerry at the annual general meeting in the midst of
this controversy. 'Next year I'd like to see more European
Roses entered for the final, especially from Germany and
France,' she declared immediately afterwards. 'Kerry has
some firm links in the industrial sphere with Germany at
the present time. In addition, with the advent of the
Common Market, it is important that the Festival assumes
more importance in Europe.'

Financially, the 1971 Festival had been a success. The
committee cleared almost all of the £700 debt from the

previous Festival. At the end of 1971, it was overdrawn by just £352, and there was £132 owed to the committee, according to committee treasurer Tom Hennebery. The total spent by the committee was £17,616, but this did not count the sponsorship of various events, which brought the total cost to around £345,000. Of that money, the committee raised £34,750 from its various dances, social functions and the Festival Club, while another £33,950 was raised in subscriptions from the town. Guinness contributed £34,700, and Bord Fáilte £34,250. The banks in Tralee estimated that the Festival brought around £400,000 into the town that year.

The Tralee committee held its 'Organisation Day' for the next Festival on 30 January 1972. There was some talk about who should host the selection. Margaret Dwyer argued that Brendan O'Reilly should be given a second chance. 'He was faced with a formidable task last year,' she contended. She and Nanette Barrett had met him in Dublin and he had offered a number of useful suggestions for Selection Night. He suggested that two girls could be interviewed together, which would ease the strain on both the girls and the compère. He also suggested that, if he got some background material on each of the contestants, he could bring them out more on stage. But O'Reilly was not available that summer: he was covering the Munich Olympic Games for RTÉ. O'Reilly was replaced by another television personality, Michael Tuomey, who had became famous as Cha, part of the double act 'Cha and Miah', on *Hall's Pictorial Weekly*.

In order to boost the publicity surrounding the arrival of the Roses in Dublin, it was decided to try to arrange an audience for them with President Éamon de Valera, but this request was rejected on the grounds that such a meeting would be inappropriate. Following the Bloody Sunday outrage, in which fourteen civilians were shot and killed in Derry on 30 January 1972, and the burning down of the British Embassy in Dublin a few days later, the prospects for the ensuing tourist season seemed particularly bleak. Eamonn Ceannt, the director general of Bord Fáilte, asked Margaret to have Linda McCravy, the 1971 Rose of Tralee, do some promotional work; Bord Fáilte agreed to cover Linda's expenses. In fact, Margaret was offered a job with Bord Fáilte, but this would have necessitated her moving from Kerry, so she turned it down.

Linda McCravy returned to Ireland in May 1972 for a two-week tour of the country and a visit to Britain. She attended the Rose Selection dances in Dublin and Waterford, as well as the Birmingham selection. Margaret accompanied her, and the two also went to a highly publicised dinner of Kerryman's Associations in London.

While in Dublin, Margaret met David Hanley, who was then working for Bord Fáilte. Hanley, who became a well-known television interviewer and presenter of RTÉ's popular current-affairs radio programme *Morning Ireland*, seemed to exorcise the ghosts of the frustrations of working for the Irish tourist board in his novel, *In Guilt and In Glory*, which was apparently heavily based on his experiences in Bord Fáilte. In the book he had a woman character with a Brooklyn accent as the president who ran the fictional 'Cahirciveen Carrot Queen Festival'. She was described as 'a third-generation returned Yank named Mrs Amelia Line, known to locals as "the Widdah Line".'

He was clearly writing a parody of the Rose of Tralee. For instance, in the book, the judges of the contest based their choice on 'uprightness, intelligence and personality, for the virtues of a good Carrot Queen were those not of the professional beauty, but of the good housewife.' The winner of that fictional contest was awarded 'the Golden Carrot'.

After President Éamon de Valera rejected the request to meet the Rose contestants, the Taoiseach, Jack Lynch, was approached, and he readily agreed to meet them. A photo opportunity was arranged with the Roses in the Taoiseach's office, and thereafter meeting the Taoiseach of the day became a regular feature for the contestants.

Having successfully exploited the popularity of folk music, the Festival expanded its efforts to appeal to the broader Irish diaspora: this approach held out the best prospect of attracting visitors in the midst of the unsettled climate in the North. A Federation of Kerryman's Associations was set up at the Earl of Desmond Hotel in Tralee on the opening night of the Festival. The patrons selected were Dr Eamonn Casey, then Catholic Bishop of Kerry, and Charles Gray-Stack, the Protestant Dean of Ardfert. Some two hundred people representing different centres came for the formation of the new federation. That number included a group of seventy people who travelled from London. Notwithstanding the almost total collapse of the tourist sector around the country, a great crowd turned up in Tralee.

'We've never had anything like this since the Festival began in 1959,' Margaret Dwyer told Tom Hennigan of the *Evening Herald*. 'Our big problem is accommodation.

The party coming with the Swiss Rose didn't book. They left it too late, and now there's weeping and gnashing of teeth. There hasn't been a bed available for Festival Week for the past three weeks.'

The Festival had already arranged bookings for some 700 visitors from the United States. This included the 128 boys and girls of the South Hedley Tiger Marching Hundred, a high school band from Massachusetts. They had raised the money to pay their own fares to Tralee, where the Festival Committee undertook to provide for their upkeep in private homes during their stay.

'How much more, and how much more loudly, can I trumpet the merits of the Rose of Tralee, that jewel in the crown of the Festival of Kerry,' Terry O'Sullivan asked in 'Dubliner's Diary' in the *Evening Press*. 'Every year I marvel at just how they can fit one more Rose on the stage, but this year there are four more – from Germany, France, Holland and Switzerland.' There was also a Rose from Hawaii for the first time. She was the great-great-granddaughter of an emigrant from Kerry who arrived on the islands in a whaling ship in the middle of the previous century.

Eamonn Casey made news by speaking out against the violence in the North at a Festival luncheon. 'Children will be made completely un-Christian and inhuman,' he said. 'The present generation is being destroyed by the total disregard for human value, by brutality and bestiality. It is building up immunity to the horror of death. I would urge you to do your best to understand that in the present unhappy situation in which this country finds itself there should be no misguided sympathy for what is being

193

perpetrated in the name of justice and peace, even though these are two things that everyone wants.' As one who had spent most of his ministry working among the Irish emigrants in Britain, he praised the Festival for drawing people together and creating bonds with emigrants. 'These are some of the small things that make it easier for the union of Europe to become possible,' he said. 'And you are well ahead of the EEC with your Roses from Holland, Germany, France and Switzerland.'

Bishop Casey was very supportive of the Festival, which had eyed his predecessor with fear, not because of anything he had done, but because the clergy tended to look on the Festival with some suspicion and because there was a danger that, if the local clergy turned hostile, the bishop – a reserved and conservative individual – would probably support them. Once the Festival was accepted by the Irish clergy in England – of whom Eamonn Casey was a member before he was appointed Bishop of Kerry – it simplified the task at home, because little survived – and nothing thrived – in provincial Ireland in the face of hostility from the local bishop. The social climate in Kerry changed markedly with the advent of Eamonn Casey as bishop of the diocese in the late 1960s.

Each year Bishop Casey held a concert to raise funds for charity in Tralee. Some of the leading entertainers, especially those who had spent time in England, volunteered their services. Most of the arrangements were undertaken by a local committee, which included some leading Protestant business people. There had been no sectarian trouble in Tralee, but over the years the main trading families were Protestants. There was a sense that it was easier for Protestants to gain promotion within certain firms, and the two communities tended to socialise separately. Bishop Casey's concert committee did more to break down those barriers than anything else. He was a man who was well ahead of his time. He was accessible and willingly endorsed the Festival of Kerry by posing for photographs with the Rose of Tralee. In his own way, both wittingly and unwittingly, he probably did more than anybody to expose the sanctimonious hypocrisy within the Church and break down the public's fear of the Catholic bishops.

The number of Rose contestants in 1972 – twenty-nine – was another record. They came from eight different countries: there were eight Roses from the United States, seven from the United Kingdom, three from Australia (from Sydney, Melbourne and Adelaide), one each from Canada, France, Holland and Switzerland and the remaining seven from various Irish centres.

At that time, Maeve Binchy, who had yet to win international distinction as a novelist, was reporting for the *Irish Times*. She made her first visit to the Festival in 1972 and was pleasantly surprised. 'The girls' schedule make an American presidential campaign look like a country ramble,' she wrote. 'Everyone has a viewpoint. There is what a respectable Tralee matron calls a "rough element" in the town as well. It arrived on the evening train on Friday, complete with sleeping bags, guitars, a lot of long hair and a few quid for beer.

'The Festival cost around £45,000,' Binchy continued. 'It attracts around 100,000 people to mill around the streets and to spend money in the town. There is a circus, there's the band of the Southern Command, there are pipe bands, variety shows, clay-pigeon shooting, tricycle races, rugby seven-a-side matches, an art exhibition, Latvian folk displays. There is something to do every minute of the day. There are people who don't know that any of these things are going on, because they are hung up on the dog show, or waiting for the Roses, or because they have never come out of the pub since they arrived.

'There were press receptions where they all tried to think of something new to say to the press, who were all trying to think of something new to say about them,' she went on. 'It's loud, and noisy, and vulgar, and sometimes pointless, but for the people, it's a success, as always.'

'It's four o'clock in the morning, and I have a column to write,' Tom Hennigan wrote in his 'Going Places' column in the *Evening Herald*. 'Not easy to marshal words, clauses, sentences and paragraphs while out there in the street, the evacuation from Dunkirk, an all-Ireland final, a stampede of buffalo and a Le Mans motor race are all going on at one and the same time. This is my first dispatch from the "War of the Roses", here in Tralee. And right now I'm envying the chaps who are quietly and placidly reporting the Vietnam conflict. Compared to me, they've a soft job. For the sounds out there defy description. It's a cacophony of incoherent shouts, disjointed snatches of song, demoniacal laughter, hysterical greetings and farewells, slamming of car doors, stuttering engines and tooting horns.'

Of course, such reports were saturated with hyperbole, but they did convey a sense of the emotion of the Festival.

The writers were obviously intoxicated of the atmosphere around them.

The new folk groups introduced that year were Perkonitis, a troupe from Latvia, and a Bavarian brass band, Messel-wang. They played in the streets during the day, along with the other bands and Bernard Ferns, or 'Fernie', the Punch and Judy man. He was a ventriloquist, novelty magician, balloon-modeller and maker of novelty hats. He moved about the streets intriguing children. It was his fourth year at the Festival. 'Why do I return year after year to the Festival of Kerry?' he said to one reporter. 'Because of the great craic on the streets and because the Festival of Kerry always pays me more than I would ever ask for myself.'

The Rose Selection was the centrepiece of the festiv-ities for many people. The Ashe Memorial Hall was packed to overflowing. Hundreds of people were unable to get tickets, so the proceedings were also shown live in the nearby CYMS hall on closed-circuit television. By this stage, the columnist Terry O'Sullivan had repeatedly been asking when RTÉ would televise 'this most photo-genic occasion which seems to cost nobody anything.'

RTÉ had made a short black-and-white film about the 1971 Festival but had made no effort to cover any of the proceedings in colour. As the station had already televised the Castlebar Song Contest, O'Sullivan argued that the selection of the Rose of Tralee would be even more suitable for television, because it had some much colour and glamour. 'The difference between the Festival of Kerry and other festivals is that this one comes from the heart, and this is something that neither money nor youth nor age can buy,' he wrote.

Eurotek Ireland, a private company, was enlisted to film a colour documentary of the Festival. Paddy McLintock of RTÉ produced it. The film contained an interview in which Margaret Dwyer outlined what the judges were asked to look for in the contests. 'A pretty girl, intelligent; she must have poise and personality and, of course, a sense of dress,' she explained. 'The judges are not looking simply for a beauty queen, rather a girl typifying the ideal of Mary O'Connor, the original Rose of Tralee.'

It fell to Margaret, as president of the Festival Committee, to announce the 1972 Rose of Tralee. The slip of paper given to her by the judges did not have the young woman's name on it. Normally when she could not remember a name Margaret would just call the person 'Honey', but she could not do that there. 'I don't know her name, but it is Switzerland,' she announced. Claire Dubendorfer of Switzerland was the 1972 Rose of Tralee.

Dubendorfer was the London-born daughter of a Dublin mother and Swiss father. She had entered the contest in Switzerland after reading about it in *Die Frau*, a women's weekly magazine. Margaret recalled that she was a lovely girl – and a bit of a flower child. She had arrived at the Swiss airport on the back of a motorcycle in sandals, with flowers in her hair. The Festival's Swiss organiser, a local travel agent, insisted that before he would hand over the ticket she had to go home and dress more conservatively. She did – and won the contest.

As usual, local people had their own explanation for why the successful Rose won. Each year people would come up with different reasons, each reason more far-fetched than the last. In Dubendorfer's case, people said it was because Ireland had just voted to join the EEC. The fact that Switzerland had nothing to do with the EEC was irrelevant to these people. After the week in Tralee, Claire returned to Switzerland, and the Festival Committee never heard of her again.

In December 1972, Margaret was nominated as Tralee Urban District Council's representative on the board of Cork/Kerry Tourism. She was to spend eight years on the board in all. In the early years it was not the happiest of boards, because there were some serious staff problems that took about three years to resolve. It seemed that, once somebody was appointed to a semi-government body, it was extremely difficult to remove them, regardless of the provocation.

Many of the founding generation had begun to outgrow the Festival of Kerry. It was time for the younger breed to take over, but many of the old-stagers were hanging on, rejecting the ideas and proposals of the younger members. It was time to take some of the younger members on board in a meaningful way. At the Festival AGM in February 1973, Margaret was re-elected president, but this time she was to share authority with a chairman, Denis J. Reen, a thirty-two-year-old dentist, originally from Millstreet. He was to assume most of the executive functions in relation to the Festival. Richard O'Sullivian, a young veterinary surgeon, was also brought onto the seven-member board.

Denis Reen was a brilliant organiser who was to inject new life into the Festival over the next few years. Many new members were introduced, and changes were made very gradually. The media coverage of the Festival in 1973 was again very positive. 'Until you have seen Tralee in the full bloom of the Festival of Kerry, you don't know what the word "festival" means,' Terry O'Sullivan wrote following the Dublin press conference announcing the Festival line-up. Bord Fáilte estimated that spending in Tralee topped £3 million during that year's Festival.

Each year, the editors of the Dublin daily newspapers would send skeptical reporters down to Tralee. They did not expect much of the Festival, with the result that they were usually pleasantly surprised by what they found. 'I had this idea that I wouldn't like the Festival. After all, women editors don't approve of beauty contests, and the Rose of Tralee is a beauty queen, isn't she?' Janet Martin of the *Irish Independent* wrote from Tralee during the 1973 Festival. 'For me it was the first one, and I reckon it will be five weeks before I catch up on the sleep I have been missing.'

'It is extraordinary, it really is. It's hard to catch the atmosphere in words,' Christina Murphy reported in the *Irish Times*. 'There is a fantastic selection of free street entertainment which ranges over magicians, Joseph Locke, Na Filí and the Chieftains. Even the circus is free. Crowds everywhere even at four o'clock in the morning. The sheer professionalism of the organisation was staggering.'

The Festival Committee had sixty-eight voluntary members, with satellite committees in Australia, Britain, Canada, France, Germany, New Zealand, Ireland and the United States. Those people made their own individual contributions – some more than others. The logistics of the Festival were staggering. Margaret Dwyer's main contributions were in the areas of promotion and sponsorship, which had a high profile, while others provided

Trojan service behind the scenes – especially Paddy Mercier, who was in charge of the stewards, and John Kennedy, who was responsible for organising the street and town-park programme. Some of the men seemed reluctant to work for a woman, and Margaret got tremendous support from her friends Nancy Caball and Nanette Barrett. The latter played a major role in arranging the dances around the county.

'It is the great fraternity of Kerry people throughout the world that has made the Festival of Kerry truly international,' Margaret explained in an article for that year's Festival. 'There is something else too – it is that indefinable thing called "atmosphere", which can waft the spirit of a song into the spirit of a Festival, a gathering, a welcome-home, call it what you like. Kerry has it because the people of Kerry have it, and because the Festival of Kerry is truly of the people of Kerry, the Festival of Kerry has it!'

Maybe only an Irish-American could be that sentimental about Kerry, but there was no doubt that Margaret's words reflected her feelings, because she believed the Festival owed its success to a whole range of Kerry people, not just in Kerry but around the country and even around the globe – people like Finbar Cox in Limerick; Bart Cronin, Tim Dennehy, and Paddy Moriarty in Dublin; Pat Daly and Mary Rose Teehan in Chicago; Harry Milner, Dermot Hussey, Tom Kennedy and Carl Sugrue in New York; Kerry Murphy in Sydney; and Eoin Kennedy in Toronto. There were also other people who had no connection with Kerry but still provided invaluable help, such as Arthur Wall, Martin Dully, Joe

Malone, Bobby Howick, Tony Prendergast and Brian Browne, as well as Joe Delaney in Las Vegas.

'Beauty competitions are bound to be a bit corny,' Christina Murphy noted in her *Irish Times* report on the Festival. 'In fairness to the Rose of Tralee, it is better than most. They do appear to judge more on personality and charm than on looks.'

Brendan O'Reilly of RTÉ was the compère for a second time in 1973. 'At least two with smart answers left poor Brendan O'Reilly at a complete loss for words for at least fifty seconds,' according to the *Irish Times* report. Interviewing twenty-seven young women under enormous time constraints was an extremely difficult task. Just three minutes was allotted for each interview, as the selection was supposed to be completed in a couple of hours. Crowds gathered in the street outside the hall to see the new Rose of Tralee.

Margaret Dwyer stepped down as president of the Festival Committee in November 1973 but remained active on the committee, taking over as honorary secretary. She received a very nice letter from Dan Nolan that she treasured. 'I doubt if the people of Kerry, and of Tralee in particular, know how much they owe to yourself and Florence, for your leadership, initiative, enterprise and energy, since the time when I had to bow out through illness, early in the 1960s,' Nolan wrote. 'Going on my own modest experience of the organisation, I know full well what the office of president of the Festival of Kerry entails, and consequently I know better than most others the debt which is due to Florence and yourself. I am linking his name with yours, at this juncture, because it was the qualities of leadership so much in evidence by both of you which had brought the Festival from the small beginnings to its present importance.'

Margaret would take particular pride in her role in the election of Denis Reen as chairman of the Festival Committee in 1973. In view of the demand for tickets for the Rose Selection, talks had already got under way for the Festival Committee to obtain its own place, in the form of a massive marquee, before Margaret stepped down as president. Reen completed the negotiations leading to the purchase of what became known as the Festival Dome – a massive tent that could seat over two thousand people.

Gay Byrne was introduced as compère for the Rose Selection in the Dome in 1974, and he subsequently persuaded RTÉ to cover the selection live on television. It seemed like a huge gamble at the time. 'The format is simple,' Byrne explained. 'It really should not work at all, but for some reason it does work, and works beautifully, and I believe part of the attraction is that it's not a beauty contest, and any of those girls could be your daughter, or my daughter, or your niece, or my niece, or your sister next door, or whatever.'

In addition to working on sponsorship throughout the year, Margaret used to look after the judges and Gay Byrne during the Festival itself. From the outset, Gay's professionalism became apparent. Just arriving on the night was never enough for him. He would come down several days in advance to talk to all the Roses individually. He would then generally know what to expect on the night. When he remarked to one of the judges that it would be difficult to get much out of one of the contestants, the judge told him that he thought she had great potential, so Gay interviewed Máire Ní Chinnéide again to discover what figurative button he should push on television. The ensuing television interview was one of his most memorable. When he reviewed forty years of the Festival of Kerry in 1999, he singled out that interview for particular attention.

In the early 1980s, when in her sixties, Margaret Dwyer was approached by the directors of the Mount Brandon Hotel, John Byrne and Billy Clifford, to take over the post of sales manager for the hotel. She agreed to do it on a part-time basis, but it turned out to be a labour of love to which she devoted her full-time attention. The job involved her travelling to Bord Fáilte workshops in Ireland and the United States. It was strangely similar to her life more than half a century earlier, when she had been travelling for AT&T.

Margaret maintained her links with the Festival of Kerry and, when she retired from the Brandon Hotel in her seventieth year, she became a Festival trustee and director in charge of sponsorship. She was present at Kerry Airport in Farranfore when the first flight arrived from the United States, just as she had been present at La Guardia Airport in New York when the first passenger flight took off for Ireland half a century earlier, for what would become known as Shannon Airport.

Tralee's only tourist attraction back then was the scenery of the hinterland, but a tourist infrastructure was gradually put in place from the early 1960s. The Festival of Kerry demonstrated the tourist potential of the area, and some people who had been very active in the Festival played an influential part in building this infrastructure. The first significant step in this area was the building of the Mount Brandon Hotel, which had over a hundred bedrooms, followed by the opening of a tourist office. Then came the development of Siamsa Tíre (the Irish National Folk Theatre), the building of a new golf course in Barrow, the opening of the Ashe Memorial Museum and the Geraldine Experience attraction, the rapid growth in holiday accommodation, and the creation of the Aqua Dome. Of course, many people played a part in these projects, but most of the developments would never have happened had it not been for the inspiration, backing and drive of certain individuals, such as John Byrne in relation to the Mount Brandon Hotel, Father Pat Aherne for Siamsa Tíre, John Griffin for the Ashe Memorial Museum and the Geraldine Experience, and Denis Reen for the new golf course and Aqua Dome. In their own ways, each of them made an enormous contributions in changing the face of Tralee in the second half of the twentieth century.

In 1999, Tralee Urban District Council made Margaret Dwyer an honorary citizen; the title comes with the practical advantage of free parking in the town for life. Interviewed that year by Carrie Crowley on RTÉ's *Limelight* programme, Margaret noted that things had been turned around since the 1940s, when there had been a lot of poverty in Tralee. 'Now it's a vibrant town,' she recalled. 'I wish I were thirty or forty years younger.'